DANGEROUS MISTRUST

FROM THE DEATH OF FAITH TO THE
RESURRECTION OF DESTINY

TRACCI JOHNSON

CHRISTIAN LIVING
B O O K S

Largo, MD

Christian Living Books, Inc.
christianlivingbooks.com
We bring your dreams to fruition.

ISBN 9781562295691

Library of Congress Cataloging-in-Publication Data

Identifiers: LCCN 2022025735 (print)
Subjects: LCSH: Johnson, Tracci. | Christian biography--California. |
   Self-esteem--Religious aspects--Christianity. | Trust in God--
Christianity.   African American beauty operators--California--
Biography. Classification: LCC BR1725.J634 A3 2022 (print)
   DDC 277.3.08/3092 [B]--dc23/eng/20220708

ENDORSEMENTS

"This book is honest, transparent, and life-giving. To be able to dig this deep into your past and give this amount of detail with no fear of opinions or judgment shows courage and, more importantly, freedom. The Inward and Outward applications, prayers, scripture references, and biblical solutions for each problem she faced lead us all back to Christ, our solution! It is apparent that Tracci has come through victoriously and wants to see all of us free and delivered as well. What a practical way to share the gospel! Tracci shares that Jesus cares and is our solution to every problem! What the devil meant for evil God turned it around for your good! The WORLD needs this type of ministry!"

—Goo Goo Atkins
Designer and cast member of the hit reality show *Mary Mary*

"On life's journey, we all have seasons of uncertainty, fear, and needing help along the way. My prayer during those times is that God sends relief and a light to help me navigate the terrain. Tracci's book serves as that light! I pray it lands in the hands and hearts of anyone who needs help when their heart is troubled. What an incredible tool!"

—Darwin Hobbs
Worship Pastor and Gospel recording artist

"Tracci literally pours her heart and soul into sharing her incredible journey. Deeply transparent and irresistibly compelling, *Dangerous Mistrust* is an extraordinary story of love, loss and revelation that will stay with you long after you turned the last page."

—Karima Kibble
Dove Award winner, Grammy and Stellar Award nominee,
Billboard chart topping artist and entrepreneur

"Tracci's journey is what perseverance looks like with grace and class holding on to faith. Through every disappointment, trial, and struggle her faith in God increased. This book will cause you to pause and do a self-check. It demonstrates what it means to do the work to heal yourself. God bless you."

—Clint and DeAnna Lewis
Authors of *Faith, Family, and Franchise*
Franchise owners of Wingstop and Fatburger brands

"I've always known Tracci to be a very compassionate and introspective woman. In *Dangerous Mistrust*, Tracci is able to passionately articulate the wisdom she has developed from her life's experiences in a way that is beneficial to others. She is able to write with a level of transparency that will challenge her readers to do the type of self-examination that is truly transformative."

—Shaun Robinson
American television host, author, producer, philanthropist, television personality and actress. She is perhaps best known for hosting *Access Hollywood* and *90 Day Fiancé*

"It is with great pleasure that I endorse *Dangerous Mistrust*, written by my friend of over thirty years, Tracci Johnson. I have witnessed Tracci's journey up close and personal, yet I am taken aback by the uninhibited transparency she shows in this book. I believe her willingness to expose her vulnerability to help others will be a transforming force for many who read this book."

—Shirley Strawberry
Co-host of the *Steve Harvey Morning Show*

"Tracci is a true woman of God! She doesn't just talk the talk; she walks the walk! I want everyone to get *Dangerous Mistrust*. It will change your life."

—Shanice Wilson
Singer, actress, and co-star of the hit reality show, *Flex and Shanice*

"In her book, *Dangerous Mistrust*, Tracci shares a litany of challenges in both her personal and professional life. The fact that she can write 'I delight in the fact that God sees my heart and He is a God of another chance,' is a triumph in itself. *Dangerous Mistrust* will bless you!"

—Kriss Turner Towner
Writer/producer of *Something New, Black Monday, Soul Man, Bernie Mac, Living Single, Everybody Hates Chris,* and *Greenleaf*

"As your Pastor, I can't tell you how proud I am of you. I have seen the hand of God on you through your many dangers toils and snares. I have seen your consistent love for the Lord. I am so proud of you. As your friend, I have watched you and admired your sincerity and resilience and strength. I have been on the sidelines cheering you on. I am president of your fan club! I am so proud of you. As your brother in the Lord, I have seen you grow, I have seen your faith stretched and mature. I am so proud of you. As the husband of your friend, Togetta, we have prayed for you, hurt with you, and rejoiced with you. You are an amazing woman. We love you. I am so proud of you. As a writer, you don't write a book to make money, or even to gain fame. You write a book because you are PREGNANT with a word for others to read and hear. I pray the Lord will use this work to bless, encourage, and inspire others to fall in love with the God you love, and the God who always loves you. I AM SO PROUD OF YOU, TRACCI."

—Bishop Kenneth C. Ulmer, Ph.D., D.Min.
Senior Pastor of Faithful Central Bible Church, Los Angeles, CA

"This book is nothing short of real talk and the truth setting you free. It is truth telling in its greatest form. I can say this because I've watched you get up every time you were torn down. I have watched you love God more and more. Continue to trust God. He is your real joy and strength."

—Togetta Ulmer
First Lady of Faithful Central Bible Church, Los Angeles, CA

CONTENTS

FOREWORD

Tracci paints a picture of relational conflict, spiritual warfare, decisional miscalculations, all to reveal a self-portrait of the tension between resilient faith in the God who loves her, and the flawed realities of the loves she lived with. She takes the reader on a journey through the battlefield of love. Tracci bears her heart as a wounded warrior turned healer who wears her scars and bruises as trophies of triumph. Having been sifted as wheat in the sieve of distorted love, she emerges to strengthen and encourage her sisters and brothers. She not only reflects on the pain of love but the power of the God who loves her past that pain.

Tracci takes you on a pit-filled path of pain punctuated—unashamedly and unapologetically—with biblical benchmarks and periodic rest stops of introspection and application. She accomplishes all of this with an unflinching gaze on her spiritual GPS. She displays a constant and consistent love for her Lord who persistently recalculates her love journey through the valleys of flawed affections and blinded perception. The Lord gently leads her back to His unfailing love, without rebuke but with the deeper revelation of His love for her.

Her greatest love affair is a spiritual one with the God who loves her unconditionally and is never frustrated by her sequential, passionate quests for true love in the earth realm. She is ultimately driven by love for her God; He keeps correcting her course back to Himself. He keeps loving her through the meandering trails of deception, over the hills and through the valleys of her earthly love search.

She takes the reader from several altars of sincere decisions to multiple agonies of deception, deceit, and depression. Tracci never sinks so low that she could not look up and look to the God who reminded her that His love never fails and that He is still with her.

Tracci is a brave, bold soldier of faith. She gently takes your hand as she retraces her steps through the battlefields of love. She reflectively leads you on a journey from hurt to hope, failure to faith, tragedy to triumph—a journey marked by biblical signposts and practical application. As a battered soldier of love, she takes you in and out of seemingly safe foxholes, only to receive continual incoming enemy fire from the one sharing her foxhole of love! And yet as a passionate reservoir of the spirit of Maya Angelou, she declares, "and still I rise." You will get angry, you will cry, you may cuss, and then you will shout, rejoice, and praise the Lord with her... until you turn the page into the next battle. Her head is often metaphorically bloody but spiritually unbowed—at least only bowed in submission, with persistent faith in the victorious love of her Lord.

—Bishop Kenneth C. Ulmer, Ph.D., D.Min.
Senior Pastor, Faithful Central Bible Church, Los Angeles, CA
Senior Advisor on Community Reconciliation to the
President of Biola University

PREFACE

> "So He humbled you, allowed you to hunger, and fed
> you with manna which you did not know nor did your
> fathers know, that He might make you know that man
> shall not live by bread alone; but man lives by every
> word that proceeds from the mouth of the Lord."
> (Deuteronomy 8:3 NKJV)

A public figure made this response to a question asked during an interview, "I don't consider myself a religious person, but I do believe in God." I remember wondering exactly what he meant by that statement and wishing I could have a conversation with him. I would ask him exactly what he believes about God. Does he believe some of the stories he's heard about Him, or does he believe God, and what God says about Himself? Does he think that his belief in God secures him a place in Heaven, or does he even believe in Heaven and hell? Or maybe, his statement was just an attempt to appease the conscience of one who has not given God much consideration?

It is expected that unbelievers don't trust God, they are called unbelievers for a reason. But how significant is it when believers are selective in their trust of God? How does their mistrust impact the way they live their lives? What blessings do they forfeit? How does it hinder their service to the Kingdom? And if we trust God for some things but not for others, are we calling God a liar with our mistrust?

Some Christians trust God for the eternal benefits of being His child but mistrust Him for the benefits available to them in the here and now.

They trust God that one day they will walk the streets of gold in Heaven but are now walking asphalt streets and concrete sidewalks in perpetual defeat. They live in spiritual poverty because of their self-imposed limitations on God. But why? What is the reason for not being our best, not giving our best, and not receiving God's best? A *dangerous mistrust* of God is at the heart of the problem.

Trusting God in some areas and not in others, is indicative of a person whose ability to trust God is dictated by circumstances. When we trust God with little problems, but panic and search for solutions outside of God when facing big problems, we are not trusting God, but the size of our problems. To really trust God, requires trusting the integrity of God—every word that comes from His mouth, no matter our circumstances. Circumstances change, but God remains the same—yesterday, today, and forever.

I want to share my story to highlight the waste of time, waste of resources, and waste of blessings we suffer when we fail to put our complete trust in God as He reveals Himself—the all sufficient One! If you are trapped in *dangerous mistrust*, I plead with you to take God at His word. Cry out to the all-knowing, all-powerful, and ever-present God who loves us with an unconditional love.

INTRODUCTION

"This is what the Lord says: Cursed is the person who trusts in mankind. He makes human flesh his strength, and his heart turns from the Lord."

(Jeremiah 17:5 CSB)

I've never considered myself a writer of any kind before. I cannot honestly say I ever particularly enjoyed writing anything. So, you might ask, where did I get the nerve to write a book? The only answer I can give is God gave it to me. I started to sense God's revelation that all the trials, pain, and heartaches I've experienced (mostly caused by me) were not just for my spiritual growth or to draw me closer to Him. But just maybe, I could encourage someone else to trust God a little more and avoid some of the mistakes I've made. I could have easily overlooked this revelation, but one night, God woke me up nine times, and each time, He gave me a thought that I wrote down. By morning, I had nine thoughts, which correspond to the nine chapters in this book.

When I felt that the book was complete and ready to be released, God kept holding me back from doing so. The longer the delay, the more God restructured what I wrote and how I wrote it. I literally re-wrote most of the book three times. What I thought was a two-year project turned into seven years. There were times when I announced to friends that the release of the book was imminent, but God said *no, not yet*. There was more for me to experience and more to learn. I needed to develop a deeper trust in God regardless of the circumstances I would face.

It is never what we experience in life that is the deciding factor, but it is our response to those experiences. I had to learn to *trust God* in a way that goes beyond just believing certain things I heard about Him. To do that, I had to acquire experiential knowledge of Him and develop a deep abiding personal relationship with the God of the Bible.

After years of struggling with low self-esteem, insecurities, self-loathing, and sometimes not wanting to live another day, I came to understand I was living my life with a *dangerous mistrust* of God. You may ask why I said *mistrust* instead of *distrust.* That's a good question because there is a difference in the two words, although sometimes they are used synonymously. Distrust can have an experiential origin caused by someone or something—being lied to, being mistreated, being neglected, being devalued, or being disappointed. It is impossible to distrust God because there can never be an experiential origin for not trusting Him. Mistrust of God

lacks experiential origin and is rooted in flawed perceptions and unsubstantiated beliefs about who He is. Because my foundational beliefs about God were flawed, everything I built on that foundation was flawed also.

After God exposed my mistrust, and I understood the origin of my flawed perceptions, He took a wounded little girl in the body of a woman, and stretched, pounded, bent, and twisted until He reshaped me like a potter's hand reshaping clay. He broke me down and stripped me of my self-sufficiency. He shined the spotlight of the Holy Spirit on all my dark, ugly, festering wounds, and would not allow me to ignore them anymore. He led me to open the door to all areas of my life that I had not made accessible to Him before because I was afraid to look at them myself. I began to understand that although I was His born-again child, since the age of eight, I spent many of my prime years living with a *dangerous mistrust.*

Maybe you will find yourself in some part of my story. My desire is to challenge you as a believer, to rise to your rightful place as a child of the Almighty God, joint-heir with Christ Jesus! I challenge you to stop walking in defeat and stop behaving like a part-time Christian. Instead, take your authority as a full-time warrior for the Kingdom. Do not just talk the talk but walk the walk. Stop being a part of this generation that engages in *dangerous mistrust.*

Much Love,

Tracci

Chapter One

A MATTER OF THE HEART

> "My son, pay attention to what I say, turn your ear to my words. Do not let them out of your sight. Keep them within your heart, for they are life to those who find them, and health to one's whole body. Above all else, guard your heart for everything you do flows from it." (Proverbs 4:20-23)

As the jailer slammed the jail door closed, I just stood there with my back against the cell door, frozen in time. As I surveyed my surroundings, all my senses were heightened—the smells, the sounds, and the sights. Everything was surreal as I focused first on the disgusting smells—body odor, vomit, and a strong presence of feces. The muffled sounds were punctuated by someone demanding to be let the (F word) out of here, and another person coughing like she had tuberculosis. I scanned the cell and stopped at what looked like a prostitute glaring down at me from the top bunk. She was dressed in all her prostitution finery and as she gave me a disgusted look, she rolled over turning her back to me. I remember thinking she was dead wrong if she thought for one minute I belonged in here with her. My eyes fixed on a small steel toilet, exposed for all to see; then I understood where the very strong smell of feces was coming from. The toilet was stopped up and waste had spilled over the sides, pooling around the base. Fecal matter was floating on top of unflushed water. I gagged as I flopped down on the lower bunk. "Oh Lord, have mercy!"

I lay there feeling every coil and spring on what seemed more like a cheap throw rug than a mattress. The blanket was useless against the cold—I was freezing. I put my arm under my head for fear there were bed bugs or lice sharing the bunk with me. I didn't sleep a wink the entire night as images of the last few hours played over and over in my mind. I hadn't eaten since Wednesday night, and now, it was just before daybreak on Friday morning. I was sick to my stomach as my head was pounding with a steady rhythm. I tried to retrace the steps that landed me in this place. How did Tracci Johnson, child of God, law-abiding citizen, get here?

My ex-husband was a very angry man plagued by insecurities. Central to many of his problems was the bitterness he expressed about how his mother emasculated his gentle-hearted, hard-working father. These family dynamics were very impactful on how he related to people in general, and specifically, how he related to me. He had little trust in or respect for women and put all women in the same category.

In many ways, my ex had the potential to be a gentle-hearted, hardworking man much like his father, but he seemed driven by a determination not to emulate his father. No one was going to slight him or disrespect him in any way. His perception of the smallest infraction, especially on my part, could send him into a rage, followed by the silent treatment. There were many times when I was clueless about what provoked him because he had a very difficult time using his words to express his feelings. But he was very good at rattling off profanity-laced sentences full of fury but little information.

During this marriage, social media was relatively new. It was and still is a great way to network and advertise your business, and I took full advantage of it. Many men, who apparently didn't have a life, were fueled by the excitement of having access to so many women through their profiles. Some men sent me indiscriminate, unsolicited, unanswered, messages. It was obvious from my profile I was married, but that didn't stop them. Because of their actions, I was subjected to repeated accusations and angry outbursts from my ex. The fact the messages were from men I didn't know and who didn't know me didn't matter. Knowing that I was abstinent before we married should have given him a clue about the type of person I was. In fact, he told me the day we married, he married me because he respected the fact that I was the one woman who said "no" and meant it.

After being married for a while, I had the opportunity to enter a lucrative partnership with a businessman to open another salon at a second location on Melrose Avenue. I knew my husband had to agree before I could even consider this venture. He met the potential partner, asked a lot of questions, and then agreed the venture was an excellent opportunity. He was involved in the planning from the beginning.

As the date of the grand opening approached, my husband started showing increasing signs of hostility toward my male partner and the business venture, in general. By this time, hours of planning had been done, lots of money spent, documents signed, advertisements in full bloom, caterers engaged, flowers ordered, business cards and stationery printed, and the grand opening date set. But now, he wanted to get agitated, confrontational, and accusatory. Even when I was single, I would not have been attracted to this business partner. And there was never a hint that he was personally interested in me.

The Thursday night before the Friday night grand opening, I got home about midnight. There was nothing unusual about me getting home that late. I didn't work on Saturdays, so Thursdays and Fridays were my busiest days. This Thursday was particularly busy since I wasn't working the Friday of the opening. Then, there was a 30-minute commute in the Los Angeles traffic.

As I walked up to the house, the lights were on as usual. I entered the house and walked to our bedroom. The door was locked, so I knocked and then called out to him several times. I could hear the sounds of the television coming from the room, but I got no response. Could he be hurt, passed out, or something worse? I called his cell phone and heard it ringing in the room. Now, I was sure he was in there, and something had to be wrong. I banged on the door and called out to him again several times before trying a credit card, knife, and a screwdriver to open the door. In a final attempt to get in before calling for help, I bumped against the door with the weight of my body several times before it popped open, leaving a dent in the wall from the impact of the doorknob.

Before I could focus my eyes to see him in the dark, he charged at me like an angry bull, grabbed me hard around my neck, and started dragging me by the neck to the guest room. I was scratching and clawing at his hands trying to make him let go. He shoved me into the guest room and told me that was where I'd be sleeping. When I questioned all this drama, he snarled, "Ask that blankety-blank you are f------!" Then he grabbed my cell phone and slammed it against the wall shattering it. In my line of business, that's like cutting off my lifeline.

As he stormed back to the bedroom, I realized he was more out of control than usual because he had put his hands on me. This was a first. I went downstairs and called the police on the landline. The police came and listened to my story, then they went upstairs to talk to him. When they came back down, one officer told me to turn around and handcuffed me. "You are under arrest." What? I'm standing there with my clothes torn, marks around my neck, and *I'm* going to jail?!?

The police repeated the story my husband told. He said I flew into a rage because I thought he had another woman behind the locked door, and when he wouldn't open it, I broke the door down and attacked him. Of course, the dent in the wall from the doorknob and the scratches on his hands served as his evidence. Because I had marks on my neck, they arrested him too.

Never in my wildest imagination would I have envisioned this scene woven into the fabric of my life. Me, Tracci Johnson, child of God, celebrity stylist featured in magazines and television shows, upscale salon owner, sought after hair expert, and fashionista, now being paraded out of my house with neighbors lined up to witness my walk of shame. One thing is certain, God is not impressed by my worldly accolades, and He will practice tough love when necessary to teach me lessons that only He can.

Earlier that night, I had entered my house dressed like a beauty queen. Now, I was coming out looking like a crackhead. I caught a glimpse of myself in the mirror by the door. My hair was standing all over my head, and my face was smeared and streaked by my mascara and tears. One false eyelash was hanging from one corner and the rest floating across my eye. It moved whenever I blinked. With my hands cuffed behind my back, I couldn't remove the eyelash or try to fix my hair. My new summer dress was torn at the shoulder, and one of my bra straps was broken, so one heavy breast hung there with no support. Oh, the shame of it all!

The police put me in one car, and my ex in another car parked parallel to the car I was in. I was crying hysterically as I looked over at him. Somehow, I expected to see some indication of regret for the trouble he had caused—some sense that he had mistakenly taken things too far. Surely some part of the marriage vows meant something to him. But when I looked at him, to my dismay, he was "wagging" his tongue at me, reminiscent of the children's taunting song, "Na-nana-nah-nah" that is often accompanied by sticking out the tongue. In an instant, I saw Satan looking back at me, gloating, applauding his victory in convincing me I could somehow win in life while mistrusting the counsel of God.

The very thing I wanted to avoid the most, happened anyway.

During the ride to the police station, my mind was flooded with images of all the warnings God had given me not to marry this angry man. But no, I didn't trust that God only wants the best for me. That would prove to be a dangerous mistrust, but I needed to maintain control over my relationship decisions. In my flawed perceptions, maintaining control was necessary to minimize the possibility of being disappointed or hurt. But on my own, I married a man who not only cared nothing about protecting me but was also gloating while bringing me down. The very thing I wanted to avoid the most, happened anyway. I was in a relationship with someone who didn't value me. My heart broke!

The police had waited until some friends came to get my dog before taking me to jail. I also gave them money to bail me out and buy me a new phone. I thought they would be able to bail me out that same morning because it was around 2 a.m. on Friday, but I was booked and left in a freezing holding cell. The benches were metal and there was no blanket—nothing between me, dressed in a thin summer dress, and the cold metal. I remember thinking how the city was wasting taxpayers' money running air conditioners when it was already too cold in the building. Adding to my shame, the police took a mugshot of me looking like I had been on an all-night binge.

When I found out I couldn't get bailed out the same morning, I was further traumatized. I had to wait to go to court later that day. I was told

I was lucky because had I come there on the weekend, I wouldn't have gone to court until that Monday. And I would have been transferred to Los Angeles County Jail, which was said to be worse than where I was. I couldn't imagine how that was possible. Even though my case was thrown out and the court appearance was canceled, I wasn't released until 4 p.m.—the same day as the grand opening. The festivities were almost over when I arrived.

What did I take away from this jailhouse experience? Like many experiences I've had over the years, the lessons learned weren't fully apparent immediately. Some lessons have been cumulative and contributed to changes over time. But from this experience, I realized that both my ex-husband and I had severely wounded hearts before entering the marriage. After dealing with our own wounds, there was nothing left to contribute to a healthy marriage. Much like him, I was plagued by flawed perceptions of my worth, even my worth to God. These flawed perceptions were caused by hurts that hadn't been addressed, and as I looked through a distorted lens, my perception of God was distorted.

I never sought a Christian counselor and I had never really discussed my issues with anyone else. I tried to confide in a couple of people, but the truth is most people don't want to help you bear your burdens. In fact, they just don't have time for your problems. Scripture tells us to bear one another's burdens, but that takes more of a sacrifice than most people are willing to make. Suffering in silence only compounded my issues, and Satan had a path of little resistance as he sought to demolish me. He got much of the raw materials he used in his deceptions from my childhood experiences. Those experiences contributed to how I saw the world and impacted how I processed information. I believe that the origin of my flawed perceptions about myself, and eventually about God, started one crisp December day in Fresno, California.

THE WAIT

My father was not a real part of my life past my first birthday. After the divorce, he would stop by every now and then, just long enough to make some grandiose unsolicited promises he never kept, and I don't believe he ever intended to keep. In fact, anyone other than a young child would have known that some of his promises were not even possible to keep. If it wasn't one of his failed promises or his obvious dismissiveness of me, he would find some other way to deposit grains of negativity into my mind. His few, brief periods of showing up always had an adverse impact on me. His actions toward me would eventually erode my ability to trust and would greatly undermine my self-esteem.

I was already having a very diffi-cult time with self-esteem issues in school. I was being bussed to integrate a school almost ten miles away, where I was the only black student in my 2nd-grade class.

Me at 2 or 3 years old.

I didn't understand the dynamics then, but the teacher was a racist and she would single me out to embarrass me in front of the class. Being a very shy child anyway, this was particularly traumatic for me. For instance, she'd make me stand in front of the class because I was late, even though I was riding on a school bus that made me late. I'd just stand there and cry while the kids laughed at me. In retrospect, she made statements to convince me I was always at fault, and my mother would be upset if she knew. So, I never told my mother how I was being treated. I really didn't understand how wrong the teacher's treatment of me was.

Another time, the class was busy rehearsing for the Thanksgiving play, but I was the only one sitting at my desk. Then the teacher announced to the class to dress nicely for the performance the next day. I put on my best Sunday dress—a fancy long dress. I don't know why I thought I was going to be in the program, but the fact that I didn't practice with the class didn't register. The teacher had me, the only black student in the class, pushing tables and chairs across the floor by myself, serving as a stagehand in my fancy dress. I didn't know how to interpret her actions as a problem with her, all I could see was that there was something wrong with me. In retrospect, not telling my mother how I was being treated probably kept her out of jail because when I told her after I was grown, she wanted to check and see if the teacher was still alive, so she could look her up. We discovered that the teacher had recently died.

I can clearly remember when I was seven years old, and my father promised me a bicycle for Christmas. All my close friends in the apartment complex were getting bikes too. On Christmas Day, I bolted to the living room when I heard my father's voice at the door, but when he came in, there was no bike. In fact, he had no presents at all. The only mention of a bike was when he stood in the middle of the living room, wearing his expensive suit, with a diamond pinky ring on both hands, bragging about how he bought his girlfriend's four kids new bikes for Christmas. I couldn't even form the words to ask about my bike. When my mother questioned him about why he was standing in the middle of her living room telling me about bikes he bought for someone else's kids and didn't have one for his own kid, he quickly concocted one of his stories. "Oh, Daddy's got a very special present for you. I just couldn't bring it today. Daddy's bringing you a horse." I totally missed the part of the story where my mother pointed out the absurdity of his statement, especially since we lived in an unfenced apartment complex. I totally missed the fire that must have been in her eyes because he had the nerves to drive all the way to our house to do further damage to my fragile self-esteem. All I heard was that my daddy was bringing me a horse—a special gift for his special little girl—his baby girl. The logistics of his promise went way over my 7-year-old head.

My mother tried not to bad-mouth my father for my sake, but Lord knows she could have. She just let me figure things out for myself as

much as possible. Most children are capable of figuring things out for themselves and need to be spared the deliberate trashing of a missing parent. Sometimes a sketchy relationship with the absent parent can, under the right circumstances, be better than no relationship at all.

Me at age 8, the year I was introduced to racism.

During the three days leading up to the arrival of my horse, my mother tried in vain to soften the disappointment I was about to experience. She attempted to provide reasons why having a horse was too much work for a little girl, but nothing she said dampened my enthusiasm. My daddy was bringing me a horse! Hooray! I told my friends in the complex and even their taunts of disbelief did not dampen my excitement.

On that fateful sunny day, I got dressed in my favorite dress. I can still see that long yellow and white gingham print dress. I sat on the porch from early in the morning—waiting for my daddy to bring my horse. I strained to see through the windshield of every car that passed, even cars that looked nothing like my father's car. Thinking about it now, I was just looking for his car; the concept of a horse trailer never occurred to me. A couple of times, I stuck my head in the front door to yell, "I think I see him!" Of course, it was wishful thinking, motivated by increasing anxiety. A couple of kids rode their bikes by and made snide remarks about me not getting a horse. I would not even leave my post to eat breakfast, lunch, or dinner. My mother served me

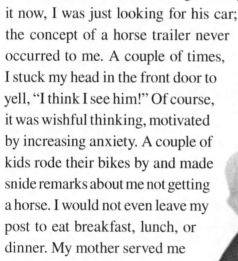

That fateful day... Me at age 7 in my favorite yellow gingham dress.

on the porch, but I really didn't have much of an appetite. I wouldn't even go to the restroom until my mother agreed to wait on the porch. I couldn't take a chance of missing him.

As the hours, yes, hours passed, my guarded optimism started to turn to panic. I can remember the feelings I had as if it was yesterday. A dark foreboding engulfed me. I became increasingly nauseous, as my stomach began to tie up in knots. My breathing became shallow as fear gripped me. I had a "waiting to exhale" experience years before Terry McMillian wrote her well-known novel that became a popular movie. Is it even necessary for me to say it? He never showed up or called. He never even acknowledged the promise of the horse. It was as if I was so insignificant to him, he could tell me anything without giving any thought to my feelings. Why would he do that? Why was I so unimportant to him that He could make a promise to his little girl, which he knew he had no intention of keeping? He could buy bikes for his girlfriend's kids, and even tell me about it, but leave "unworthy me" with nothing. Why didn't their own daddies buy them bikes? According to my father, each one of them had a different daddy anyway. Maybe if my daddy hadn't gotten all those bikes for them, he would have gotten one for me. I couldn't find a suitable answer to any of my questions other than there must have been something wrong with me. That wasn't the last time his promises didn't materialize, even though I kept trying to believe each new promise could possibly be the one he would keep.

TWISTED PATTERNS

I didn't know it at the time, but that day of waiting for my horse would shape my responses, not only to real disappointments but more importantly, to anticipated disappointments, for years to come. A destructive pattern was formed out there on that porch. Those same feelings I felt that day would engulf me every time I faced the possibility of being disappointed. I would have the same dark foreboding feelings. I would become nauseous as my stomach tied up in knots. My breathing would become shallow as fear gripped me. I also erroneously *learned* over time, the only person I could trust to care about my innermost feelings was me.

If a man I was interested in made a commitment to do something, even if he kept his word and arrived on time, I would have died a thousand deaths while waiting for his arrival. My vivid imagination would take me to a place of disappointment, and I would cry like my world was coming to an end before it was even time for him to arrive. I had destructive real-life reactions to imagined heartbreaks and disappointments. There were times when I was legitimately disappointed, but the degree of my disappointment was far greater than what was reasonable, given the depth or lack of depth of the situation. My reaction to real or imagined disappointments was always mingled with the pain of my childhood disappointments. I couldn't separate the past pain from what was presently going on. Ironically, for reasons that didn't make sense, I usually got involved with men who fueled my expectations of disappointment. Expectations of disappointment became a part of my comfort zone.

I had destructive real-life reactions to imagined heartbreaks and disappointments.

My reaction to anticipated disappointment wasn't just limited to relationships. If I anticipated something good happening in any area of my life, I could get physically ill while waiting for it to materialize. Often, before that "good thing" happened, I would sabotage it because I needed to put an end to the agony of the *wait*. At one time, I was the hairstylist for the once very popular group, En Vogue. When we traveled in the United States, I could tolerate the plane trips, although

I was afraid of flying. But one day, En Vogue gave me the opportunity to go on a European tour that would hit many major cities. Who wouldn't see this as an exciting adventure? I agreed to go, but I was in a deep panic agonizing over a plane crash that was a certainty if I got on the plane. I wasn't fearful the plane would crash if I wasn't on it. In fact, I expected everyone else to arrive and return home safely. I knew it didn't make sense, but what I knew in my mind was not compatible with what my emotions were telling me. So, I missed out on a great trip. En Vogue went on tour and returned safely home. It was years later that I made it to Europe, on my own dime.

Over the years, I've learned to really appreciate how we are admonished in scripture to guard our hearts. Everything about us is influenced by the condition of our hearts.

> As water reflects the face, so one's life reflects the heart.
> (Proverbs 27:19 NIV)

The experiences of a person raised by a warm, attentive father could easily transition to an image of a warm, attentive Heavenly Father. But I was exposed to an erratic toxic father who treated me like I didn't matter, so you can understand my difficulty in transitioning to an image of a warm, attentive Heavenly Father. Can you see why that may not have been possible for me, since my only experiences associated with the word "father" had been negative ones? Nevertheless, after we receive Christ as Savior, God's purpose is to make us progressively more like His Son. Some of our journeys are more difficult and time-consuming than others.

The healing of my heart didn't come by one swoop of God's mighty hand, but it came in increments fueled by disappointments and hardships, many I caused myself. Still, along my journey, I recognized God's faithfulness. Even now, when I face discouragement, sometimes I must go to my Heavenly Father for reassurance He's got me.

Me with En Vogue while on tour with them.

Contrary to what some may teach, all newborn Christians don't hit the ground running for the Lord. I couldn't run a fruitful race until I shed some of the emotional baggage that was weighing me down. I am still learning and still shedding baggage as I am being matured in Christ.

Some people can't run effectively until they get a broader understanding of what being saved by grace through faith in Jesus Christ means. I had to learn that it is more than a ticket to Heaven; it's about allowing Christ to work in me to live out heavenly principles in the here and now. It's about being on the mountain tops and in the deepest valleys yet trusting in the God of my salvation. It's about embracing my failures and victories in my everyday life as I am being progressively conformed to the image of Jesus Christ.

A.W. Tozier, one of the great Christian preachers of the 20th century, stated, "What you believe about God is the most important thing about us." God invites us to intimacy as His children because He wants us to seek His face and His heart. In His invitation to intimacy, He gives us some added incentives.

> Call to me and I will answer you and tell you great and incomprehensible things that you do not know.
> (Jeremiah 3:33 CSB)

These great and incomprehensible things are reserved for people who seek intimacy with the Lord. It really is a matter of the heart!

INWARD APPLICATION

Reflect: Have your views about the nature of God been consistent, or have they changed over the years? How were your views formed initially, and how have they changed? What factor played a role in any changes?

OUTWARD APPLICATION

The world is full of people who have difficulties envisioning a Heavenly Father way up in Heaven who loves them because they have no point of reference. For many, the association of the word "father" with the word "love" is a foreign concept. What if God's people everywhere would commit to no longer taking a band-aid approach to evangelism—a pat on the back and a matter of fact, "God loves you", and do a revolutionary new thing? (Sorry, that's a little sarcastic). What if we ask God for a heart to seek out the unsaved, the disenfranchised, and the unhappy wherever we find them, and let Him show His love for them through us?

Pray as you look around intentionally to see how you can show love to someone.

PRAYER

Lord, I desire a more intimate relationship with You. Help me to slow down and seek Your face with all my heart. Also, show me new ways to be useful in Your Kingdom as I allow You to love others through me.

For anyone who has not received Christ as your Savior or anyone not sure of your salvation, I refer you to Chapter 10, "The Invitation". God loves you and has a plan for your life.

Chapter 2

EXCUSE MY HUMANITY

"He brought me up from a desolate pit, out of the muddy clay, and set my feet on a rock, making my steps secure." (Psalm 40:2 CSB)

In 1986, the British pop band Human League recorded a hit song entitled, "Human". This song was written by acclaimed songwriters Jimmy Jam and Terry Lewis and was a big hit on the music charts. Lyrics of the song tell of an exchange between a man and a woman who only recently reunited after a break-up, and they both confessed to being unfaithful during their time apart. In essence, they were saying, "Excuse my humanity—I couldn't help it. I had to fill the emptiness somehow."

This song reflects the attitude, not only of non-Christians but also professing Christians—the ongoing attempt to find someone or something to fill the void in their hearts. You can be a born-again Christian and still experience emptiness if you have not yet experienced *yieldingness.*

People try to fill their emptiness in various ways: alcohol, drugs, sex, food, other people, careers, material gain, status, church work, volunteer work, good works, etc. I was convinced that only a husband and a couple of kids could do it for me, but it wasn't the husband and kids that I desired, as much as it was what they represented. They represented a certain status that said I was somebody worthy of having a husband and kids who loved me.

When I accepted Jesus as my Savior at age eight, I didn't understand the concept of His Lordship over my life, or my need to yield to His guidance. I found it easier to trust Him for the salvation of my soul than to trust Him for day-to-day control over my life. So, the battle began! I was searching for a human solution to the spiritual problem of my emptiness. I was looking for a human solution to my lack of worth and validation. I didn't understand until years of futile searching that only an intimate relationship with the God of my salvation could fill the emptiness lingering in my heart and give me my sense of worth.

UNREQUITED LOVE

I don't fully understand the origin of it, but I had this fantasized view that being married and having a couple of children was the best life had to offer. However, I don't think my first love relationship was birthed out of that fantasy but out of the pure love of a young girl's heart. My first love relationship was when I was 18 years old, and it served to reinforce an already fragile self-image. And it set me on a destructive path to fill a void I thought I could find in my humanity.

I met this young preacher when he visited our church from a neighboring church. Even though he wasn't what most young girls would call physically attractive, in my young mind, he had a charisma and a swag about him that would rival Barack Obama or maybe even Denzel Washington. I know that's saying a lot! He was extremely gifted spiritually and had a way of endearing himself to people. In Biblical knowledge and the ability to articulate that knowledge with clarity, he was light-years ahead of most people, young and old. This wasn't my imagination, but it was substantiated by the many accolades from older pastors and the fact that he was highly sought out as a guest speaker. In addition to all his many good qualities, he treated me like I really mattered. He was at our house often, and my mom and I would go hear him speak whenever possible. I couldn't get enough of him.

After a beautiful start, by the end of the third month, I sensed that something wasn't quite right in our relationship. He was physically there, but it was obvious that his mind was preoccupied. He seemed particularly distracted and troubled just before we were to attend a state-wide church convention where members from both of our churches, and several other churches would be in attendance. Since he was playing a major role at the convention, I was looking forward to watching him so eloquently carry out his responsibilities.

He didn't show up or call for the two days before the convention, which was not like him. Of course, I told myself that he was busy preparing for his convention responsibilities. However, just an hour before we were to leave for the convention, I received word that he had gotten married the day before to a girl from his church who was pregnant with his child. Now, the change in his mood made sense. I went numb; then the reality started to set in. Words fail me in capturing how deeply I loved this man or the depth of the pain I experienced during this, my first heartbreak.

Not going to the convention was not an option. My mother was the Youth Director for our church and supervisor of our youth, so she had to be there. Plus, she would never let me stay home alone for three days. I didn't even have time to digest the news of the marriage or to grieve before we reached the convention. I tried to pretend I was okay, but it felt like I could barely breathe. It was impossible not to see him since he was one of the moderators, but now, I found no pleasure in watching him carry out his responsibilities. I vividly remember having to sing in the choir the first night of the convention, while trying to fight back my tears, but they flowed uncontrollably.

To make matters worse, and they did get worse, out of all the rooms in this very large hotel, my mother and I ended up in the room next to his room. What are the odds of that? His church made the arrangements for their members, and our church made the arrangements for our members. I felt like I was the object of a cosmic joke in the Heavenlies! He had no idea we were next door to him until later the second night, but I knew he was next door from the first night. I wouldn't have known except he was always loud and animated and had this distinctive laugh that I easily recognized. It was surreal when I heard that laugh ring out every few minutes as he talked with his friends. How could he be so happy while I was consumed with pain? Why couldn't he at least be quietly happy? The awareness that God had allowed this situation to happen felt as if He was mocking me, along with certain girls who were gloating as they asked me about the rumors that he was married. Why God? What terrible thing did I do to deserve this? You knew this was going to happen, so why did You let me get into this relationship? Don't You care? Don't I matter to You? Where do you run for comfort when you stop trusting God?

> **Where do you run for comfort when you stop trusting God?**

On the second night of the convention, after we had settled down in our hotel room, there was a knock on the door. My mother opened the door—it was him. She let him in because she knew that I needed closure, and she instinctively knew that he was hurting too. I was sitting on the bed that was the farthest from the door, and he sat on the foot of my mother's bed, closest to the door. After a few words, he suddenly buried his face in my mother's lap and started wailing loudly like his sorrow came from the depth of his soul. He apologized and said the pregnancy happened before he got with me, but he was informed of it more recently after the girl's parents found out. He talked about how conflicted he was because of all the pressure he had received to do the *right thing*. He didn't want to marry, but he was convinced by others that he had no choice, especially because he was a young minister, and the girl was a member of the same church he attended. At that point, I didn't doubt that he loved me, but a wrong deed before we met derailed any hope for our future, and there was nothing that could have been done about it.

The year of the worst heartbreak of my life.

That night began a saga of unrequited love in me. That painful experience impacted my life for many years to come. His memory took on a mystical quality in my 18-year-old broken heart, and for years, he outshined any other man I met. This man received my love in its purest form—free, trusting, and unguarded. But I was left with a need to protect my heart from ever experiencing that level of hurt again. From that experience, I also fell into a trap of twisted thinking about God, and how He valued me as His child. I believed He loved me enough to save me as a part of the "world" He gave His only Son to die for, but He was not particularly concerned about me individually. I didn't understand it then, but I was starting to view God as one who abandons and disappoints, reminiscent of my earthly father. Because there were flaws in my foundational thinking about who God is, everything I built on that foundation was flawed too. Before long, I found myself in a downward spiral of going through the motions of Christianity, looking like I had it all together, but there was a serious disconnect.

CONUNDRUM

Dr. Tony Evans used the word "conundrum" in a sermon I heard on YouTube. The sound of the word piqued my interest, so I looked it up to get a clearer understanding. One of the definitions is "a paradoxical, insoluble, or difficult problem, a dilemma." What a perfect word to describe how I lived my life for years in the strength of my humanity! On one hand, I wanted a knight in shining armor to swoop down and rescue me—to cover and protect me—to validate my worth. However, I was too afraid to get involved with men I thought could and would be able to carry out those tasks. If I really fell in love with a man who qualified, I would be positioned for serious heartbreak because I couldn't keep that type of man. My sense of vulnerability was staggering! During most of my twenties and thirties, I lived with this conundrum—wanting what I was afraid to have, even though I had no trouble attracting what I wanted.

Perhaps the following story will clarify the reality of my dilemma. At one point while I was on tour with a recording artist, I met this wonderful man backstage. There was an instant connection between us, and we had the most effortless and meaningful conversations and spent hours talking, whenever our schedules permitted. Initially, I didn't know what role he played on the tour, or why he was even there. I knew his name, but I didn't know the accolades associated with his name. He was just a very nice guy that this girl enjoyed being with. I didn't know he was well on his way to being one of the biggest names in the music industry. When I learned who he was, the news came from someone who thought I already knew, and just mentioned the information in passing. But for me, red lights and sirens went off! Immediately, I started to shrink back to that little girl whose father rejected her—that little girl who wasn't enough.

All the negative self-talk about how I could not possibly function in his world flooded my mind. The fact that I was already functioning just fine, escaped me. I pulled away from him and sabotaged any potential for a relationship, solely because of my fears—not because of anything he did or did not do. He didn't change—he remained who he was when I first met him. What changed was my perception of myself as it related to the new information I had about him. I lost my ability to just be me—the same me that he had enjoyed spending time with—the same me that had enjoyed spending time with him. Suddenly, I was inadequate—not enough. It wasn't just that I felt inadequate, but I was inadequate.

For as he thinketh in his heart, so is he. (Proverbs 23:7a)

My actions reflected my negative thoughts about who I was. I have no way of knowing if this was a relationship that could have developed into something lasting, but the point is I ran away from what could have been what I said I wanted because of my negative thoughts of myself.

KNIGHT IN NOT SO SHINY ARMOR

About three years later, not long after I moved to Los Angeles, I met a young screenwriter and movie director. He was an up-and-coming name in the movie industry. He represented one of those knights in shining armor types I was afraid of, but he pursued me hard, and I decided to take a chance. Thinking back, it would have been better if I had run away this time too. Even though I got into the relationship, I was still operating from a place of *not being enough*. Seeing myself as inadequate made me susceptible to allowing myself to be treated like an option, instead of a priority.

We started out making beautiful memories—going to different events, sightseeing, and spending quality time together. He never seemed too busy for me. But after a while, as we were excitedly waiting for the premiere of his next movie, he started being a no-show without even calling. Then when he did show up again, he would not even mention the broken date or promise. Each time he went missing in action, even though I was deeply hurt, I would not confront him. I would always revert to that little girl who sat on the porch all day waiting for her no-show daddy to bring her a horse. At least, my boyfriend did show up—sometimes days late, but he did show up.

When my man pretended he did nothing wrong, I pretended right along with him. I made excuses to myself that he was very busy preparing for the release of his movie. I was excusing the fact he was treating me like an after-thought, and I was taking it. It should have been obvious he was taking me for granted, but I was just glad that he showed up at all.

As the premiere date neared, I made meticulous plans about what I would wear on the red carpet as I walked beside my man. I tried different hairstyles and shopped for the perfect shoes. I chattered excessively with my customers about this big date, and my man allowed me to chatter with him about making sure that my color scheme didn't clash with what he was wearing to the premiere. Then on the day of the premiere, he picked me up in a limousine along with his family. When we arrived at the premiere, he got out and left me with his family. He did not allow me to walk on the red carpet with him—no explanation, just a complete revision of what he knew I was expecting. I was fully aware that a spirit of cussing would have manifested in many women, and they would have blasted him in front of his parents, then demanded a ride back home. I am not saying that would have been a proper response, but something in between would have been better than how I handled it.

Later, during one of the few times I questioned his actions, I gingerly asked for an explanation. His excuse was that only the people associated with the movie walked on the red carpet, and no one had their significant other walking with them. Since he had me seated with his parents instead of with him, I couldn't see what took place on the red carpet. Still, I have watched enough red-carpet walks on television to know that what he told me didn't make sense. After all, he was the director of the movie.

Now, I know that you are waiting for me to tell you how I exploded and told him to get lost. But no, I buried my head in the sand and allowed myself to be disrespected in this relationship once again. He apologized and wanted to make it up to me, so he planned a special outing for us to Catalina Island—just the two of us. We planned a special gourmet lunch menu and he told me to buy the ingredients, make the preparations, and he would give me the money back. I had three days to prepare for our outing. I purchased a cute picnic basket, expensive food items like smoked salmon, got a new dress, sun hat, and sandals. I even had my nails re-painted to match my dress. (Even as I am writing this, I could kick myself in the behind for this foolishness!)

I waited for hours, but he did not show and did not call. It just so happened that my mother was in town during this time, and I was so distraught that I couldn't hide it. After talking to her, I grew a temporary backbone, and when he called—three days later, I was ready. He did not mention the trip or the fact that he stood me up. No apology, no explanations, no regrets. Finally, after so many of his no-shows, I said enough is enough and told him goodbye in a not-so-nice way. If my mother hadn't been there to talk me through it, I may have buried my head again. Sometimes we need someone to hold us accountable when we are drowning in nonsense. Oh, I later found out from a reliable source that this director was sleeping with at least two women associated with his latest movie. In retrospect, I don't even know what I saw in him anyway. His actions showed he was not a man of integrity, and he was never too good for me, as I felt then. If anything, I was too good for him. Looking at life through dirty lenses distorted my perception of everything including who he was, and who I was.

BEEN AROUND THE WORLD

By my mid-twenties, I was on a mission to find a husband—my only way to find validation. I didn't have the sophistication to understand I was looking to replace a missing daddy and the fairy tale family I envisioned as a child. Attracting men was never a problem for me, and I've had more than my share of opportunities to marry. But even though I was consumed with the search, I was prone to getting cold feet and backing out. People, who knew me well, were surprised when I finally followed through and got married the first time.

Not that I made a conscious decision, but after the experience with the movie director, the type of men I involved myself with greatly changed, and the conundrum of my life took a radical shift. After years of Christian counseling, and developing an intimate relationship with the Lord, I can be introspective and brutally honest concerning my relationship mistakes. I can see one common factor prevalent in the men who came after the director—it was my perception that they needed me in some way.

I needed to be needed more than I needed to be loved.

At some point, I abandoned my search for a knight in shining armor. I evolved into this woman who was so self-sufficient I didn't bother to pray to God for a husband anymore. I could make things happen for myself, or so I thought. I could not only take care of myself, but I also assumed the role of the one riding in on a white horse to save the day for any man I was romantically involved with. Who's going to leave me if he really needs me? Being needed became my comfort zone, my place of empowerment, my security blanket. I needed to be needed more than I needed to be loved. Why? Because if a man needed me, I had value and a means to hold him. Because I couldn't function well in a relationship with a man I could end up needing, this was the answer to my problem.

If a man didn't have himself *together* professionally, emotionally, financially, or spiritually, I was the *fixer*. If he needed to be in therapy and wouldn't go, in charged Tracci, the therapist, who couldn't even help herself, but had all the answers for him. If he needed a better relationship with the Lord, in charged Tracci, Bible in hand, willing to do missionary dating while her own relationship with the Lord was dismal. If he needed a wardrobe update, in charged Tracci, the stylist—running all over town shopping to do a make-over whether he wanted it or not. If he needed family support, in charged Tracci, ready to share her supportive family who, at least on the surface, accepted anyone acceptable to her. If he hadn't identified his purpose (and maybe he wasn't even looking), in charged Tracci, spiritual counselor, pulling and tugging, leading the way, while obviously oblivious to her own purpose. If he didn't feel good about himself, in charged Tracci, the cheerleader, complete with pom-poms, willing to dim her light to help him shine. I even went so far as to link someone with average credit to my credit to improve his credit. It's hard to admit, and I didn't understand why I was doing what I was doing while I was doing it, but if I could somehow enhance a man's life, he would see value in me, and not leave me.

I purposely did everything with kindness—with a focus to build up, not tear down, because after all, who *needs* someone who is not kind. I also cooked these wonderful meals to increase my value, but at least I had sense enough to get them to contribute to the grocery bills. I saw my actions as standing by my man while making myself indispensable to him. And to be honest, most of the time, I was more concerned about people knowing that a man left me than I was about him being absent from my life. I was only loosely attached anyway. And ironically, 99 per cent of the leaving was done by me, after putting all that effort into keeping the men.

I will be the first to say that my reasoning was extremely flawed because men who needed me always resented needing me, and at some point, in some way, they rebelled against my help. No matter how kind I was, in the end, I was subjected to some form of abuse— manipulation, control, attacks on my character, or weaponizing my vulnerabilities. As I said before, I was prone to get cold feet and bail. Somewhere under all the foolishness, I had a few sensible moments.

Lisa Stansfield sang a hit song entitled, "Been Around the World ". The song is about a determined and confident search to find the object of her love. Before I was out of my twenties, I felt like I had been around the world looking for my love and I couldn't find him. The more desperate I got, the more foolish I got, and certainly the less I sought divine guidance. My efforts were doomed from the beginning because I was trying to find a human solution to a spiritual problem—a wounded soul that only God could fix. I would predict many people, both women and men, play themselves cheap in seeking relief from emptiness and aloneness because they don't know their worth, and are seeking validation from the wrong sources. The journey begins with believing who God says we are. To the wrong person, we will never matter, but to the right person we are precious.

> See what great love the Father has lavished on us, that we should be called the children of God! And that is what we are! (1 John 3:1a NIV)

DOXOLOGY

Just in case you may be wondering if I even had contact with my first love again, I did. Some 28 years later, our paths crossed. I believe God allowed him to resurface so I could get a new look at him through more mature eyes and be set free from the idealized version of him. And I learned a valuable lesson this time. I realized I had made him a god in my life, and I was sacrificing on the altar of his memory. Because I saw myself as unworthy of the good things in life, such as real love, I slipped into a comfort zone of pain and misery fueled by my unrequited love. Losing him gave validity to my dismal life and a justifiable reason for my perpetual unhappiness.

God had a purpose for allowing me to reconnect with him. This second time around, I realized, as a grown-up, I admired very little about him. Even many of the qualities I thought he had when I was a young girl, were the figment of a young girl's imagination. When I realized he was not that man, and there was no way God had sent him back to me for a relationship, the fairy tale ended. This time, I had no regrets. That seemingly "eternal flame" was forever out, and I was free of the stronghold that was holding my heart captive.

INWARD APPLICATION

If you are a Christian, do you have an intimate relationship with God, your heavenly Father, or is there an emptiness in your soul? Are you ready to take God at His word?

> And without faith it is impossible to please him, for whoever would draw near to God must believe that he exists and that he rewards those who seek him. (Hebrews 11:6 ESV)

OUTWARD APPLICATION

Ask God to help you identify someone: a family member, a neighbor, a co-worker, or a friend who needs a self-esteem boost. Make it a point to build that person up. For example, sincere compliments/recognition, including them when appropriate, intentionally conversing with them, joining/inviting them to lunch, phone calls just to check in, etc.

If you are not a Christian, you can pray to God and accept Jesus Christ as your Lord and Savior now. Refer to Chapter 10, "The Invitation". God loves you and wants to save you. The ball is in your court. Jesus has already done the agonizing work for your salvation.

PRAYER

Lord, please search my heart and reveal what my spiritual needs are so that I may lay them at Your feet and allow You to meet those needs. Lord, please help me identify someone who needs the encouragement that I can offer. In Jesus' name, I pray. Amen.

Chapter 3

COUNTERFEIT LIVES

"Search me, God, and know my heart; test me and know my concerns. See if there is any offensive way in me; lead me in the everlasting way."

(Psalm 139:23-24 CSB)

When I was a teenager, my mother had a close friend and colleague whose husband was the most prestigious layperson and the largest financial contributor in a mega-church. Not only did he make large contributions to the church regularly but even more so during major fundraising campaigns. He had the connections to secure large contributions from individual businesses and corporations. He was always recognized for raising the most money during those special campaigns.

This couple had a beautiful home in which they both took great pride. My mother said their house was so clean and organized it looked like a model home with no occupants. The husband was a nice-looking man, and the wife was physically beautiful with a warm, friendly personality. Her hair always looked like she had just left the salon, and her appearance was always flawless. Many of the church members seemed eager to see what this couple was wearing to church each Sunday because their outfits were always coordinated in some way, thanks to the wife. She would discuss their outfits for the upcoming Sunday with my mother at work. Their outward appearance seemed very important to her.

MR. AND MRS. PERFECT

Mr. and Mrs. Perfect were always full of smiles as they walked hand in hand to their special seats in the church. The wife would tell my mother that eyes were locked on them as they sat in the pew that had a velvet needlepoint sign draped over the back to identify their seats. They were, by far, the most admired couple in the church. But sometimes looks can be deceiving. This husband often beat his wife, and strategically hit her in places that could be covered like on her back, chest, head, or stomach. She shared her problems with my mother, who felt the covered lumps on her body. The husband also used vile, evil ways to taunt his wife with evidence of his cheating on her. As the wife shared these stories, it was never with a sense of "enough is enough."

Some leaders in the church, including the pastor and wife, knew of the husband's behavior. The pastor and first lady had taken care of the wife after some of the beatings. Still, this behavior never interfered with this man's leadership position in the church. He was never asked to step down or held accountable in any way. It was also common knowledge to some, including the wife, that the husband had girlfriends in the church who were brazen enough to disrespect the wife to her face. It didn't matter. People smiled, looked the other way, and continued to treat this couple like superstars. Maybe their support was based on the definite advantage of getting the big bucks this man contributed to the church.

The saddest counterfeit in this scenario was the wife who pretended to be a happy, well-cared-for woman when she was a battered wife.

It is difficult to understand her position in all this. She was highly educated, had her own wealth, and there were no children to be considered. Yet, she was driven by a need to receive recognition and admiration that was as false as her happy marriage. This wife's story ended sadly when she was murdered in a home invasion while her husband was out of town.

As a young teenager, I just couldn't understand how this woman would allow herself to get caught up in this counterfeit life. How was it that she did not see what others saw in her? I didn't realize it then, but many years later, I would begin to understand the ramifications of not knowing your worth and possibly why this woman became trapped in her counterfeit lifestyle.

TRANSPARENCY

I agonized over whether I would share this next story with you because it shows a level of desperation that is very embarrassing. However, if I can help someone by being transparent, I will. Remember to keep a spirit of meekness —and don't laugh too hard—considering yourself because you too may face a lapse in common sense, or maybe you already have.

As I approached thirty, none of my efforts to get to the altar had materialized, and I became increasingly anxious to be married and have babies. After all, my biological clock was ticking. I had plans that weren't coming together fast enough and, as panic set in, I fell victim to a con artist/sociopath who took a counterfeit life to a whole new level. Looking back, I am convinced I was under a demonic attack, one which I set myself up for when I chose to wander into unchartered territory without the guidance of the Holy Spirit. Satan saw me out there on my own and set a trap for me. I fell into it—hook, line, and sinker! I can imagine Satan, and his demonic host, getting a good laugh at my expense.

One busy Friday afternoon, while I was working on a client, I became aware of some whispering going on around me. The commotion was centered on this handsome man who was sitting in the barber's chair. As I glanced in his direction, our eyes locked, and it seemed like the world stopped turning for a moment. I had a waiting to exhale moment. To this day, I hope I wasn't drooling as this tall, lean, nicely dressed man caught my attention. I think every woman in the salon turned her head to look at him. We made eye contact a couple more times, and he flashed his pearly whites. I got so excited because I knew instinctively that when he finished with his haircut, he was coming straight to me, which he did. As he glided across the floor to me, he looked like the hero out of a romantic novel. After he introduced himself, it didn't take long before I concluded that he was the most amazing man I had ever met.

It was established by the end of the conversation, we would see each other again, soon. I was the lucky one that day and the envy of so many women, I'm sure. He was the talk of the salon for the rest of that day and many days to come. I started thanking God for answering my prayers because He had blessed me exceedingly, abundantly, above all I could even think to ask for—or had He? It's dangerous to make assumptions about God without checking in with Him first. Everything that glitters ain't gold!

I didn't want to take a chance on God saying, "No."

This man had a deep abiding walk with the Lord and a knowledge of scripture that fascinated me. At last, I found a man who could challenge my mind with his great understanding of God's Word. Oh, the bible discussions we could have. It was then I understood why I hadn't met the right marriage partner before—God was saving me until this man came to town! It was well worth the wait! As we developed a relationship, I never bothered to seek God about whether this was an answered prayer or a counterfeit. In retrospect, I know I didn't want to know. I didn't want to take a chance on God saying, "No." Being perfectly honest, if God had sent me a registered letter signed, "The Lord God Almighty," I wouldn't have opened it because I was in a "hear no evil, see no evil" mode. How pathetic is it when desperation sets in, and we play the fool?

God couldn't get to me with a word of caution.

I thought, if I can just keep things moving, everything will work out. Maybe I didn't form the words in my mind, but I was determined to override God and *will* this relationship to work out. After all, where was I ever going to find anyone better than this? He had everything I wanted in a man. Somehow, I thought I knew more about what and who I needed than God did. How misguided I was to think I could get what I wanted by ignoring the Spirit of the living God in me. Why did I think I could determine what God's best was for me? I was looking at outward appearances but only God can see what's lurking in the heart.

I introduced this man to family members, and he attended an out-of-town family wedding and other family gatherings with me. He was funny and engaging, could quote scriptures like a pastor, and pray like one of those old southern deacons. We had wonderfully deep discussions about the things of God and about our future in ministry. In retrospect, are you kidding me? I was going to do ministry for the Lord, the same Lord I had excluded from the relationship? I hung on this man's every word, but my prayer life and Bible study habits were being neglected. I had a black-out zone around me so God *couldn't* get to me with a word of caution. And, after all, I was getting my spiritual "food" from this profoundly spiritual man. That was how I excused my behavior. The fact that this man never once tried to convince me to engage in any sexual activities only enhanced his "godliness" in my sight. I had the nerves to take pride in being abstinent and being a faithful tither while deliberately ignoring God! I was doing like so many others do, choosing which sins I would avoid while excusing or ignoring other sins. That was dumb, dumb, and dumber! I was knee-deep in sin!

This man made it clear that he wanted to marry me, and we'd laugh and joke about "our children". I even met his 10-year-old son, and in a very tender moment, his son told me he only wanted two things in life—a dog, and me for his mommy. Boy, did my maternal instincts kick in! I had visions of baking cookies and being a soccer mom. And of course, I was going to be a card-carrying, fund-raising, active member of any parent groups at the school. I even started planning how I would decorate a room for a 10-year-old boy. It had to be spectacular!

THE OSTRICH MENTALITY

Desperation took my focus off God—His ways, His timing, and His will. To tell the truth, at this point in my life, it was like the devil had performed a spiritual lobotomy on me. My brain was like mush, and I offered no resistance to his tricks. I had not yet learned just how dangerous it was to mistrust God. Oh, but I was in the process of learning a real hard lesson! I wanted the dream of this marriage so badly I allowed that desire to drive me, instead of letting the Holy Spirit guide me. This kind of desperation opened me up to self-deception, increased vulnerability, and a loss of plain common sense. Honestly, I was way more in love with my fantasy marriage than I was with

> **This kind of desperation opened me up to self-deception.**

this man. He represented the avenue to my fantasy life; a husband and kids—status—worth.

I also acquired an uncanny ability to make excuses for any sliver of reality that slipped past my black-out zone. I had an answer for everything, and I wasn't going to accept even the possibility that what I wanted would not materialize. I call this dangerous condition the Ostrich Mentality. Although a myth originating in ancient Rome, it is a good metaphor comparing our lack of vigilance in relationships with how an ostrich will bury its head in the sand with the rest of its big body exposed to all kinds of danger. With its head buried, it's not vigilant in recognizing impending dangers.

In humans, the side effect of the Ostrich Mentality is to become deaf, mute, blind, and just plain stupid. I'm sorry to say, but I developed the Ostrich Mentality more than once in life, but the consequences were never as severe as they were this time. The Ostrich Mentality made me an easy target for counterfeits who could have been destructive to my very life, had it not been for the Lord keeping me. Satan already knew that He couldn't take my soul because I am in Christ, but his attacks were designed to render me so ineffective I would be useless to the Kingdom. But God!

SELF-IMPOSED BLINDNESS

After about four months of bliss, this man disappeared for about two weeks with no phone calls or texts. Since I was used to talking to him every day, I was so upset with him, and I promised myself that I wasn't going to deal with him anymore unless he could prove he had been in the hospital and unable to contact me. I became physically and emotionally ill in his absence, and all my abandonment issues surfaced. I couldn't sleep and I lost my appetite. I was like a zombie at work just trying to get through the day without breaking down in tears. When people asked about him, I had to pretend that everything was good, but I was just one more question away from melting into a heap of snotty tears.

Finally, he returned, looked longingly into my eyes, and told me how God had called him to shut away for a period of fasting and prayer. He said there was a tremendous calling on his life and since I was going to be his wife, we would be facing serious demonic attacks. It was his job to cover me in prayer, so when God called him to drop everything and shut himself in, he did. He was so sorry for worrying me, but He had to do just what the Lord told him to do—the price for having such a tremendous call on his life. How could I argue with God? "Oh, my God, thank You for this spiritual giant! Thank You for the favor of choosing me to be a part of Your ministry. I vow to give my all to You for Your service!" There I go again, thinking I can do ministry for the Lord without being on the Lord's side.

There were several more unexplained periods of time with no phone calls or texts. After each return, he had a story to tell. The aunt who raised him died, and there were some weekends that he needed alone time to deal with his reoccurring grief. Other times, he was away having deep encounters with God. The stories of these encounters became more and more bizarre. As my grandmother would say, "By now, I should have known that there was a dead cat on the line, somewhere." In fact, these stories would have been downright ridiculous to anyone who wasn't desperate to hold on to a fantasy. I'm too embarrassed to tell you any of these stories because when I think about my efforts to accept them, I feel really disgusted with myself. I'm just not that stupid, but when you get so far away from God that you refuse to trust Him, that mistrust puts you in much danger— totally exposed to all that Satan throws at you. God wasn't just showing me the writings on the wall, but He had neon lights flashing warnings to me. However, I just put on sunglasses and kept it moving. I refused to see anything. I refused to hear anything. I refused to know anything. I was going to make a life with this man, no matter what!

Normally, it was easy for me to talk to my mother about my relationships, even though she often pointed out the obvious that I was missing. But this time, I could only bring myself to share one of the "deeply spiritual revelations" this man shared with me. As I was telling her, the story sounded increasingly ridiculous, and I knew on many levels that nothing was real about his stories. So, I not only kept the other revelations to myself, but I stuffed them in a corner of my mind and refused to think about them. I just wanted to marry this man and have beautiful babies. I wasn't open to anyone, including God, telling me that it wasn't going to happen. I was willing to expose my future to devastation just to hold on to this fantasy.

GOING TO THE CHAPEL AND WE'RE GONNA GET MARRIED

Finally, we started planning for the wedding. A date was set, six bridesmaid dresses were purchased and hanging in the closet. The deposit was made on my wedding gown. We found a venue for the wedding, met with the coordinator, spent most of the day planning everything, then he paid the $2,000 deposit for the facility with a check. Did you notice that the payment was made with a check? You can guess what happened next. The check bounced! In fact, the account the check was written on had been closed for a couple of years. He couldn't be located by the wedding coordinator to deal with the bounced check, so I was the one she was seeking for an explanation. He did a real disappearing act this time. No explanation, no follow up, no apology, no closure—he was just gone in the wind! All I had left was the pain of knowing nothing he said was real. Again, I trampled over every warning God gave me—determined to trust my efforts and mistrust God.

Now, some of you may be asking yourself, "How could she be so wrong?" Part of the reason I wanted to share this story is because in my line of work, I've encountered many women who get caught up in fraudulent relationships, and many who have knowingly allowed themselves to be lied to, used, and abused, just to look like they have a man or are happily married. I've known women who have allowed other women to look on with envy at huge diamond rings that their men supposedly bought when they really bought their own rings. Some women allow themselves to be stripped of every ounce of dignity to live counterfeit lives because their public image is more important than their truth. Often, these women are professing Christian women who are educated, respected in their careers, financially stable, but vulnerable because they don't know their worth.

This same scenario can be true of men. Women do not have exclusive rights to not knowing their worth. The underlying reason is the same in all cases—not trusting who God says we are in Him and what we mean to Him. It's a dangerous mistrust—one that can destroy the very essence of who we are designed to be. And it can send us on a journey of lostness that some people never recover from. So, I know that I am not the only person—man or woman — who has struggled with the feeling of not being enough. The problem is one of getting information from the wrong source. We are bombarded with all types of advertisements from worldly sources telling us what we should look like, what we should be like, what we should have to be somebody. But if man's report is contrary to what God says about us...

> Let God be true and every human being a liar. As it is written: "So that you may be proved right when you speak and prevail when you judge. (Romans 3:4 NIV)

SHIFT IN EMOTIONS

I started telling this story feeling embarrassed but as I am writing this sentence, I realize another emotion has replaced the embarrassment—the need to reach out to those who are struggling. Too many men and women are suffering in the body of Christ for us, who have experienced the deliverance power of God, to keep silent! People need to see living testimonies that God can, even when we cannot. So, I just made the decision not to be embarrassed anymore. I don't want to gain admiration and recognition for being a counterfeit super saint. Instead, I want to honestly share my struggles so that I may impact someone's life for the better.

I struggled through hard trials trying to learn what some little girls learn naturally from their earthly fathers, that I have worth, that I matter. I was raised by a divorced mom who was struggling with her own low self-esteem. She was an only child, raised in an abusive home, with a father who told her she should never have been born and treated her like he meant every word. She was not taught about the love of Christ in the home, but she was active in church as a young adult. One of her unsaved friends, who was busy doing *church work* along with her, got saved one Thursday night. My mother was not present when she accepted Christ, but the friend gave a testimony in Sunday School the following Sunday morning. My mother recognized something different in her friend—something she didn't have, and she began seeking Christ for herself. Three weeks later, she accepted Jesus as her Savior. So, by the grace of God, my mother was saved almost three years before I was born.

My mother taught my brother and me biblical principles while she was learning them herself. Yet, I am saved today because she prepared me to understand the gospel at eight years old. And I've had experiences in life that would have caused some people to forfeit the race, but I'm still here, and I owe it to God for teaching me who I am in Christ. So, I'm making myself available to God for His use, imperfections, and all, because He is calling for perseverance, not perfection. Thank God for Jesus!

DISCOVERY

The break-up with the handsome counterfeit was my second most painful one, but it was quite different from the first. In the first relationship, I was an innocent victim of pre-existing factors that eventually influenced the breakup. However, this time, I contributed greatly to my problems because I chose to mistrust God and follow my own course. To this day, I'm not sure what was worse, losing the dream, or the embarrassment of people knowing what happened. I felt worthless, exposed, and ashamed.

Even though I didn't want anything else to do with this man, I wanted to know who he really was, so I gave the information that I had to my "investigator mom." She found out about his whole life in a few hours. This is what I could have and should have done from the beginning, but I didn't want to know anything that didn't fit into my fantasy. Getting information about him was easy because I knew the city and the out-of-state church he attended most of his life. That was one thing he told the truth about. My mother had a long conversation with the aunt who raised him after his parents put him out. It was the same aunt whose funeral he attended and grieved over for months. She wasn't even a little bit shocked that he told me she was dead. She said no one who knew him believed much of what he said. My mother found out that he was already married when he was with me and had previously been married before that marriage.

That sweet young boy who tugged at my maternal heartstrings lived with his daddy and his mommy in the same house—and in the same city where I lived. He evidently was being trained by his dad to be as deceitful as he was. And he was good at it! He is sure to be a danger now to any woman he meets. I'm convinced his dad carefully orchestrated all the talk about him wanting me to be his mom. In addition to all that, this man had at least six more children by different women, including a set of twins, and was wanted in two states for unpaid child support. The aunt even volunteered the names, ages, and locations of his children. Nothing about this man was true. He didn't work where he said he did, and the Mercedes he drove wasn't his, but his wife's.

> **I was a willing participant in this counterfeit relationship.**

My mother also spoke for a long time with this man's former pastor. The pastor acknowledged this man was indeed extremely gifted in biblical knowledge but was just plain no good—a con artist. He had a reputation for being a womanizer who sought women who would support him. The pastor stated before he would let this man come near his daughter, he would pack her in a box and ship her off to Africa. The advice he sent to me was, "Run, and don't look back!"

Don't you find it interesting all this information was at my fingertips, and I wouldn't pursue it? It was that doggone Ostrich Mentality! Normally, I would have gone to his house and his job at some point in the relationship, but I sensed something was wrong, but I refused to confirm it. I made it too easy for him to deceive me because I didn't ask questions, follow up on suspicions, or investigate anything. I never met even one of his friends. Yes, I was deaf, mute, blind, and stupid! I was a willing participant in this counterfeit relationship.

I have no excuse for falling prey to this smooth-talking counterfeit because I can truly admit that God was on His job! I knew that He was warning me, and I knew I was purposely ignoring Him. Once I decided to put my trust somewhere other than in God's plan for my life, I made myself a target.

> Trust in the Lord with all thine heart; and lean not unto thine own understanding. In all thy ways acknowledge Him and He shall direct thy paths. Be not wise in thine own eyes; fear the Lord and depart from evil. It shall be health to thy navel, and marrow to thy bones. (Proverbs 3:5-8)

I wish I could say that I never again ignored God's warnings, but I can't. I was a hard-headed child. There were tough lessons ahead.

I never settled in my mind the reason for this man's deception or what it was he expected to gain. He never even hinted about any money or sex, so I remain confused about his motives to this day. Maybe he just enjoyed the sport of deception, and he was a master at it. Whatever his motives were, I am convinced that he was an agent of the devil. God allowed this situation, as well as others, to teach me the folly of my outlook on life, and to draw me into a real relationship with Him. After this twisted adventure. I was consumed with self-loathing, and I exhausted my vocabulary with all the synonyms for "stupid." I had wasted time, energy, and let's not forget about the money involved in the wedding plans. Of course, Satan, the accuser, was taunting me with every detail of my bad decisions. He played back the story of my shame in my mind for weeks as I struggled with insomnia.

NOW I SEE

Now, going back to the story of my mother's friend, I have a better understanding of how she allowed herself to exist in such a toxic counterfeit relationship. Maybe, she never learned that she mattered—that she had real value. And maybe, instead of accepting who God said she was, she accepted an assessment of her worth from the wrong sources. One thing is for sure, she was operating from a place of brokenness and was a co-conspirator in a counterfeit life that never gave her what she apparently was seeking.

Sadly, the world is full of people living counterfeit lives, and far too many of them are in the church. There was a time when Christians were encouraged to look to people in the church for potential mates, and that was good advice, but now, even that needs to be more carefully examined. Just because you find someone in the church, it doesn't mean that you need not examine him or her more thoroughly. Sometimes we overly spiritualize our potential relationships and just settle for outward appearances. But we need to examine the quality of the fruit, if there be any, and stop getting captivated by the shiny green leaves on the surface. Shiny green leaves can camouflage the fact that there is no fruit to be found, and you can end up with someone who looks good on the surface but produces no fruit or fruit that is rotten to the core.

There are also people in the church outwardly displaying a level of holiness—super-saint status, that struggling Christians have no hope of achieving, but these same people may be living contrary lives in private. This can be very harmful to the growth of the church. There are also people who are so busy pretending they have it all together but are suffering inside. Yet, they are too afraid to share with anyone for fear of judgment. I remember looking around the church and wondering who I could confide in about some of my struggles without being judged. Older Christians should be seasoned and ready to walk alongside younger struggling Christians, but too many will criticize and demean them for doing things they used to do themselves. And if the truth be told, some of them would still be doing those things if they could find someone to do them with.

Do you suppose, O man—you who judge those who practice such things and yet do them yourself—that you will escape the judgment of God?" (Romans 2:3 ESV)

WASTED TIME

I wasted so many years allowing my worth to be defined by someone who didn't even understand his own worth—my father. I flew from Los Angeles to Atlanta to see him on his deathbed. There he was facing death any day, and of all the things you would think a person might talk about at the end of life, he literally started to cry about how he was mistreated by his family from early childhood. He repeated the same story he had told for years to anyone who would listen, whether they had heard the story before or not. His parents never loved him; they made a big difference between him and his siblings, and they badly mistreated Him was his story. What? Doctors say you only have a few days to live, and all you can think to talk about is how you were mistreated as a child almost 80 years ago. I stood there puzzled! The hurt was still so fresh it had him crying like a wounded little boy as he faced eternity. I had forgiven my father several years before, but if I hadn't already forgiven him, I certainly would have forgiven him that day. All I wanted to do was embrace him like you would a crying little boy to kiss away his boo-boos. That was very sad to witness.

> How can a broken person make me whole?

As I stood there looking down on him, I really saw the magnitude, and the invasiveness of that ugly monster—unforgiveness. It moves unmercifully as its tentacles invade the soul of who we are, spreading poison, shredding potential, and halting the fulfillment of purpose. It was crystal clear how I had been duped by the devil for so many years, chasing smoke as my life ran amok because I thought this man deliberately chose to withhold love and validation from me. But as I looked at him, questions began to flood my mind. How could he give what he didn't have to give? Could he pour from an empty container? How could he emulate what was necessary to provide me with a sense that I mattered when he had never experienced it? How can a broken person make me whole? What I had done all those years was look to my dad as my source, and he was depleted of anything that could help me. Not only was he not my source, but he wasn't even a resource until a court order caught up with him after I was grown and made him pay thousands of dollars in back child support. He was furious! God has always been my source, even when I didn't give Him proper credit. He was there all the time.

> Every good and perfect gift is from above, coming down from the Father of the Heavenly lights, who does not change like shifting shadows. (James 1:17 NIV)

My father accepted Christ as his Savior two years before I was born, and he accepted his calling to preach the year I was born. Because I know experientially you can be saved and not yet delivered, I do believe he was saved. He was saved because He accepted Jesus as his Savior but hadn't allowed Him to be his Lord. He was saved but never delivered because he was shackled to unforgiveness. I believe my father, like others, thought forgiveness was too good for the people who hurt him. But forgiveness is for you, not for the people who hurt you. It frees you to give love and receive love. My father never found the love he so desperately wanted and died a lonely man.

Me and my dad during his last days.

I refused to allow unforgiveness to continue to hold me captive, so several years before my father died, I forgave him. I am so thankful because I would not want to be like my father, on my deathbed still singing the same sad "Woe is me" song and being a victim. I refused to continue to parade around projecting an image that was counterfeit—looking like I was something I was not: okay. When I owned my brokenness, I was delivered because I was willing to forgive, and put my trust in who God says I am.

My goal is to live a life of authenticity so that God may use me and be glorified by my life. My prayer is that in my willingness to be authentic, God may encourage others to drop the counterfeit and embrace authenticity.

INWARD APPLICATION

Get away for a few hours and spend time with the Lord—no interruptions, no food, no electronics. Ask for help identifying areas of your life that need purging. Is there someone you need to forgive? Open your heart's door and engage God in an honest conversation about pretenses in your life, and the underlying causes. Remember, what God reveals, He's ready to heal.

OUTWARD APPLICATION

Write a letter or talk in-person to people you have not forgiven. Tell them how they offended you. Then tell them you are forgiving them whether they asked or not. Then in the power of the Spirit of God in you, let the offense and the pain go. Caution: I am not saying you should re-establish relationships with people who have proven to be toxic in your life. Forgiveness doesn't always mean reconnecting. Use wisdom. Don't kick a hornet's nest! There may be someone you would be better off not contacting, but you can still forgive.

PRAYER

Heavenly Father, please show me myself, the real one. Shine Your spotlight on the flaws and shortcomings I have either overlooked or refused to deal with. Clean away those things about me I don't want others to know because I hate them myself. Forgive me, Lord, and help me forgive myself. In Jesus' name, I pray. Amen.

If you are not a Christian and would like to be, refer to Chapter 10, "The Invitation". God loves you and has a plan for your life. It may not be easy to accept the fact that God loves you unconditionally, but if you make the effort to seek Him, He will show you His love.

Chapter 4

WHAT'S LOVE GOT TO DO WITH IT?

"He that has my commandments, and keeps them, he it is that loves me; and he that loves me shall be loved of my Father, and I will love him, and will manifest myself to him." (John 14:21)

Many years ago, well-known singer Tina Turner asked the question in song, "What's love got to do with it?" It seems people throw the word, "love" around with no real concept of what it means. Others make thoughtless decisions and damaging sacrifices in the name of this often-fleeting emotion.

I was in love with the idea of being in love. But I was more in love with the trappings I thought went with love—the perceived status that went with having a husband and kids. As I stated before, often, I cared more about being seen as alone than I cared about being alone. You know how people can ask questions like, "You don't have a date?" "You haven't gotten married yet?" I had accepted the false information that being in a "love" relationship validated me and gave me worth. Through communication with my clients over the years, I realize I'm not the only one who has accepted this false information.

I floated from one relationship to another looking for *love* in all the wrong places. Many kinds of emotions come under the umbrella of "love," but I suggest most of what the world refers to as love, is just infatuation—temporal and conditional in nature.

Agape love is love in its highest form.

Agape is a Greek word that refers to a deliberate choice to love, not a sentimental feeling. Agape love goes against natural human inclinations, but it is love in its highest form. It's the love God has for us, which He demonstrated by giving His Son to die for us. It is a love that those in Christ, through the Holy Spirit, can experience.

As children of God, we must show our love for Him by our obedience and by bringing glory to Him by how we choose to live. Glorifying God requires a genuine effort to know and represent Him well in the world. How glorifying God is accomplished differs from person to person. One person may bring glory to God from a mansion high on a hill. Another may bring glory to Him on a football field or foreign mission field. In whatever manner God wants His people to glorify Him, one common element links us together—committed hearts that love and trust God enough to accept His will for our lives. I'd like to share a story of someone who, according to the standards of the world, glorified God from a very unlikely place.

NANCY BOO

Growing up, I had a cousin, Nancy, who was very close to me in age. Most family members called her Nancy Boo or Little Nancy because she was named after her Aunt Nancy. Her parents had three adult children (all boys) before Nancy was born. This cute little girl was a star in our extended family. She had two working parents and could have all the private lessons and activities they could provide. While still a young girl, Nancy became a star majorette and performed with a nationally recognized twirling team. She had a room in her home dedicated to trophies. They were everywhere and many of them were taller than she was. At family gatherings, everyone flocked to Nancy Boo. "Hi, Little Nancy. Got any new trophies? Your room is so pretty! Nancy this, Nancy that." Those same relatives would walk past me as if I was invisible and head straight to Nancy Boo. It infuriated my mother that grown people would speak to one 7-year-old, and pass by the other one standing there, without speaking. But my mother was careful not to influence my thinking about it, and never mentioned how she felt until I was a grown woman.

We had this teenage cousin who took it upon herself to take every opportunity to point out Nancy's greatness and my ordinariness. "Don't you wish you were a champion like Nancy? Don't you wish you had all those trophies? Don't you wish you had a pretty room like Nancy Boo's?" My mother got so sick of the teenage cousin taunting me she decided to remove one of her taunting tools. One day, she took me to a furniture store and bought me the prettiest bedroom set in the store, complete with everything that was on display with it. She really couldn't afford it, and she didn't explain her reason for buying it until years later. My bedroom had everything new, and it was beautiful! I never heard from my teenage cousin again about pretty bedrooms.

Nancy was in many beauty competitions as a child and won several of them. She went on to be the only black lead majorette, ever, for her high school band. She was just good at what she did. Her career dream was to become an actress and a dancer. Family members talked about Nancy's dreams as if they were a done deal.

Now you would think that I would have been jealous of Nancy growing up, but for reasons I can't explain, I never was. Nancy was such a sweet, loving person, with the biggest grin and infectious laugh. Neither she nor her family ever made me feel devalued. She never acted as if she bought into her "greatness." I was always her first choice for sleepovers and family road trips. Our house was always her first choice as a place to stay when her parents needed a sitter.

At one time during our elementary years, we ended up going to the same school, but her family later moved to a ranch in the country by the time we were in high school. There was never a harsh word, name-calling, an argument, or hard feelings between Nancy and me. I don't remember a time when we had to be disciplined for not getting along. Nancy and I were both saved at a young age, and maybe the *God* in us connected our hearts then and for eternity.

*Me and Nancy Boo at age 7, obviously
before we got our hair combed.*

Eventually, I completed cosmetology school and was off touring with then R&B singer, Pebbles. Nancy was in college pursuing her dream of becoming an actress with a strong dance emphasis. That first summer, she landed a job at Disneyland as a dancer for one of the productions presented several times daily. One day while rehearsing, Nancy just fell and then urinated on herself. There was no explanation why this happened. She was also having periods when she couldn't see. She dropped out of school and was back home going through a series of medical tests before I knew anything about her condition.

The New Year's Eve after Nancy's fall, we were both at my house for the weekend. We went to a New Year's party someplace near Lake Merritt in Oakland, California.

Me and Nancy Boo when we were about 14. They caught me with my eyes closed.

I knew nothing about Nancy not being in college anymore, but there was one thing I particularly remember about that New Year's Eve, which only made sense after I found out about her condition. That night, Nancy danced with a sense of desperation—like she was dancing for a lifetime. She danced to every song. She danced until her clothes were drenched with perspiration. She danced until her curls were pressed against her face and the back of her neck. It wasn't like her to sweat out her hair, especially since I had it looking extra good. I couldn't fathom why, but it seemed, from time to time, she lost her balance and got offbeat. Still, she danced on and on until the very last song. Later that night, Nancy took a very nasty fall down some very steep stairs at my house. When my mother told Nancy's mother, she noticed that she seemed more concerned than expected, given the fact Nancy seemed to be all right.

About a month later, the news reached me that Nancy was diagnosed with multiple sclerosis (MS). She was already in a wheelchair by the time I saw her again. Sometimes the deterioration of MS on the body is slow, and if it goes into remission, then a person can live a normal life for years. But none of this was true for Nancy. She went down fast. Before long, she couldn't walk, she couldn't feed herself, and she couldn't control her elimination. She had to wear diapers and rely on others to clean her, dress her, and feed her. Her speech was slow and halted, and she had poor use of her arms. Even the slightest attempt to move her arms resulted in terrible uncontrollable shaking. Her head needed to be stabilized to get food into her mouth. But there was one thing that did not change—her big grin that she flashed as often then as she did before she developed MS.

Nancy lived many years with this condition. For the first couple of years, she could go to school with an attendant who assisted her. This period was very special for her, and she was so appreciative of every day. She made new plans to study in a field that would allow her to assist people with disabilities. She also looked forward to going to church each Sunday. Even with her halted speech, she frequently declared, "God is good!" Then she'd follow that up with a big grin, as her head bobbled around in a way that made you want to grab her to steady it. Someone might wonder how she could make a declaration of God's goodness in her condition. But Nancy's assessment of God's goodness wasn't contingent upon her circumstances, but on who He is and what He has already done to prove His love.

> But God demonstrates his own love for us in this: While we were still sinners, Christ died for us. (Romans 5:8 NIV)

Nancy's love for the Lord was pure and unconditional. As much as I loved Nancy, I struggled hard with my emotions concerning her condition. I avoided her whenever I could get away with it. By this time, I had moved to Los Angeles, and I'd sneak back to the Bay Area so she wouldn't know I was there. My mother, on the other hand, always had "visit Nancy time" built into my schedule. She would get upset with me when I made excuses for why I couldn't make time to see her. She said I was acting as if I didn't care, but the truth was I cared too much.

Nancy's love for the Lord was pure and unconditional.

I felt guilty I was up doing me, and she was confined to a bed and a wheelchair. Why was she in that condition while I was walking around in 6-inch heels?

In my absence, my mother visited Nancy several times a week because, by that time, Nancy's family had moved back to the city and lived in the same condominium complex as my mother. The highlight of Nancy's day was hearing some news about what I was doing in my career. My mother understood Nancy was living vicariously through me, and she would beam with delight with every report—the "Tracci reports," as they referred to them. It often took Nancy 30 seconds or more to ask a question, but my mother got used to figuring out what she was trying to say and would finish sentences for her. Nancy would say, "Yeah, yeah," as she moved her arms uncontrollably with excitement. My mother would tell her every detail she could think of and show her pictures highlighting where I was and who I was with. She also read magazine articles about me or my salon to her.

After a while, under the penalty of death by my mother, I started visiting Nancy myself. At first, even though she asked me questions, I still felt guilty telling her about my life. It seemed as if I was being insensitive to her situation. She would struggle to ask a question and I would give her a short answer. But Nancy would be visibly frustrated by my short answers because she would have to struggle to ask another question to get more information. Finally, I got it! Nancy traveled with me in her mind. She saw what I saw and met the people I met. She wore the clothes I wore, and walked in the shoes I walked in. After I understood, I began to tell her stories in detail, and she would giggle with excitement like an innocent little girl. Those were fun times we shared. She needed me, and I needed to be there for her.

There was never a hint of regret from Nancy about her condition. I know of no one who ever heard Nancy ask the question, "Why me?" She never displayed jealousy, envy, or anger toward me or anyone else. She was genuinely happy to hear about what I was doing, and she was my biggest cheerleader during the time I toured. After I opened Eclipse Salon, she had to hear about every celebrity who set foot in it. The purity of who she was produced this refreshing quality that felt like it represented all the goodness of who God is.

During the time I was on tour with Babyface, he was the heartthrob of many women, young and old. He was one of Nancy's favorites. His tour was scheduled for San Jose, California, which was close to my mother's home in Hayward. So, I got tickets for the concert, and my mother brought Nancy, wheelchair, and all, to hang out with me at the concert. It was probably one of the most exciting events of Nancy's life. She was always so much more of a "groupie" than I ever was. Backstage, she got the VIP treatment, and when the concert started, she sat with the biggest grin on her face. I am grateful we were able to do that for her.

Another time, my mother drove Nancy from Oakland to Los Angeles to see my salon shortly after I became the owner. Nancy took only one more trip to Los Angeles before her life took another drastic turn. A few months after her last trip, she choked on some food due to the failure of her muscles used for swallowing. She lost oxygen to her brain for too long and was reduced to a vegetative state. There were no more big grins and no more giggles.

The first couple of times I saw Nancy in her new condition, even though she couldn't speak, or smile, her eyes lit up, and they would follow me as I moved around

Me and Babyface while I was on tour with him.

the room. She'd look intensely in my face, more so than she did with others. I would talk to her as if I knew she understood, but as her health deteriorated, she didn't seem to know anyone. Outliving both of her parents, she lived in that state for several more years. Eventually, she died in a rest home where the Lord had given her favor with a staff of people who had grown to love her and who took very good care of her.

When the news reached the family, I believe all of us rejoiced as we pictured her dancing among the angels, basking in the love of Jesus, with that big grin on her face. Several family members admitted they had been praying for years for her release from this life, so she could be whole and healthy. We had all struggled with the question of why God allowed her to live in such a sad condition for so long. But even now, I can find comfort in this scripture:

> For I reckon that the sufferings of this present time are not worthy to be compared to the glory which shall be revealed in us. (Romans 8:18)

Several years have passed, but thinking about Nancy's life is still painful and still causes me to tear up. She had so much potential, and I wish that she could have accomplished so much more in this life. However, I truly believe from God's vantage point, she accomplished all that He set before her. Even with the telling of her story, God is ministering to someone through her life, and she is still glorifying Him. She loved Him, truly loved Him and even during her difficult circumstances, she trusted in His goodness. I can hear Jesus say...

> Well done! You are a good and faithful servant. You've been faithful over a little. I'll put you in charge of much. Come, celebrate with me. (Matthew 25:23 CEB)

The Apostle Paul instructed us to be content in whatever condition we find ourselves in. Nancy "walked out" that scripture in her lifetime.

She showed all who encountered her what that scripture looks like in action. She accepted God's sovereign will in allowing her condition, without bitterness. How does a person love God like that? It was a "nevertheless" love that was shed in her heart by the Holy Spirit. I would like to think that I could have handled being in Nancy's condition with such grace, but only God knows. I just must do my best to glorify Him on the path He lays out before me.

How does a person love God like that?

One thing is for sure, our purpose as Christians is to glorify God, and we won't all glorify Him from the same vantage point. One day, I look forward to being reunited with my cousin Nancy Boo, and we'll dance together among the angels. And once again, my heart will be blessed by that big grin on her face.

DIFFERENT PATH

My life took a very different path than that of my cousin, Nancy. We both accepted Christ as our Savior at a young age, and we were both full of potential, but I can't explain God's reasoning for our journeys in life. I've tried to make sense out of it for my own under-standing, but all I can say is God is sovereign; He can do things His way and He is never wrong.

> For My thoughts are not your thoughts, nor are your ways My ways," says the Lord. "For as the heavens are higher than the earth, so are My ways higher than your ways, and My thoughts than your thoughts. (Isaiah 55:8-9 NKJV)

Until I was about 16 years old, I had expressed interest in becoming a cosmetic dentist. I was looking at Gambling as the school to attend.

I wasn't ever sure I wanted to be a dentist, and later, I started having second thoughts because I had an interest in hair styling. My brother was already in college, and I knew going to college was expected. However, I finally got the nerve to tell my mother I wanted to be a hairstylist in the entertainment industry and didn't want to go to college. Once I got the words out of my mouth, every perceived road-block fell like dominos. My mother said she wasn't surprised because of the number of cosmetologists in our family, and the talent she saw in me. She still laughs at how I would get up extra early when I was around 5 or 6 years old so I could comb my own hair before she got to me. At first, she would take my hair down and comb it over. Then one day, she took a good look at my work and decided I could comb my hair as well as she could, so I was given the responsibility of combing my own hair.

Even though my mother received some criticism from relatives who thought I should not be allowed to skip college, she never wavered in her support. In fact, she'd let me practice cutting her hair on many occasions, even though sometimes she had to cover up bald spots with an eyebrow pencil. I really expected my brother to disagree with my decision to attend beauty school. Instead, he said, "If you're going to be a hairstylist, be the best!" His words have motivated me throughout my career. My brother sported haircuts that were often lop-sided, but he never complained because he liked the price—free.

LESSON LEARNED

I started cosmetology school before I graduated from high school. By age 18, I was working at one of the top salons in Oakland California, Center Stage West. Ron Newton, son of Black Panther leader, Huey P. Newton, was my mentor and eventually one of my best friends. Let me stop my train of thought for a moment to talk about Ron. Ron Newton was an extraordinary stylist. To this very day, over

30 years later, I have never known a stylist more talented than he. He was a good-looking man with chiseled features and wore his long hair in a ponytail most of the time. He had such a magnetic personality that it was obvious his mostly female clientele adored him. He'd have many clients booked in short spaces of time, and no one ever seemed to mind the long waits. Honestly, I think many of them enjoyed the extra time to sit, watch, and interact with him. He was a stylish dresser, who was always up on the latest trends, and he lived well. He seemed so carefree and appeared to enjoy life to the fullest. The jovial atmosphere in the salon was greatly because of him. It was not unusual for him to take a dance break in the middle of the salon to showcase his skillful rendition of the latest dance moves. By all appearances, he had it all!

One month after I moved to Los Angeles, I got the word that Ron Newton had committed suicide. It was on the exact day his father, Huey P. Newton died two years before. No one saw that coming! Everyone was in shock! I rehearsed over and over in my mind why no one saw his misery. Obviously, success and the good life on the outside can do nothing to fill the anguish within. Someone said there is a God-shaped hole inside of every person that only God can fill. That event emphasized how important it is to present the God of our salvation whenever we have the opportunity. I was young when I worked with Ron and did not have the boldness I have now to share my faith. I also did not have the level of discernment I have now. Still, I can't help but wish I had somehow known about His struggles. He seemingly had everything to live for, but life was so difficult, He ended it. His popularity, his adoring clients, and his material gains meant nothing to him. Behind the fun-loving exterior,

Behind the fun-loving exterior, he was dying inside.

he was dying inside. We can't make assumptions about the state of anyone's life. My cousin, Nancy, seemingly had nothing to live for, but she loved life, and she loved the Lord. Ron, seemingly, had everything to live for, but took his own life.

At age 19, I went on my first tour with Pebbles, a popular R&B singer at the time. She saw my work at Center Stage West and asked me to tour with her. At age 20, Dudley Hair Care company sponsored a nationwide styling contest. Two stylists from each state were selected to compete for a spot on a national styling team. I won for the state

Me and my mentor and best friend Ron Newton.

of California and went on to win at the national level to get a spot on the 10-member national gold styling team. I traveled with the Dudley Team for a couple of years before later moving from Oakland to Los Angeles, California.

After I got touring out of my system, I settled down and started to work at Eclipse Salon on Melrose in Los Angeles. This was my dream salon. It was on the second floor facing Melrose Avenue, only a few blocks from Beverly Hills. It shared a courtyard with the then, very popular restaurant, Georgia's. One of the owners of that restaurant was Denzel Washington. When I walked into Eclipse for my first day of work, I can't tell you how, but I knew I would one day own that salon. In fact, I told my assistant (now a very skilled stylist) who was walking beside me, "I am going to own this salon one day." If you ask him today, he will recall the day I claimed Eclipse Salon.

> **I am going to own this salon one day.**

Shortly after starting to work at Eclipse, I noticed that the owner was trying to sell the business. She had a couple of interested people with a sale price of $200,000, but nothing materialized. Later, she kept dropping the price until she got to $75,000 and still, nothing happened. Then, she dropped the price to $50,000 but still, there were no takers. After that, she seldom came into the salon. She had a new love interest and didn't seem to care about the salon anymore. Some people just have money like that. One day when she did come in, I just walked up to her and said, "You ought to just give me this salon." I don't know how I got the nerve to say that because I barely knew this woman. And I don't know what I expected her to say—maybe laugh in my face. But to my surprise, she said, "I can't give it to you, but if you give me $10,000 you can have it." I could have it with all the furniture, with its 10 booths, with its reputation, with its status, with its prime location, with its ambiance for $10,000! That was nothing but God!

I stood there in a stupor for what seemed like a long time, trying to be sure she had said what I thought she said. Other stylists had been working there much longer than I, but no one expressed interest in the salon because God was reserving it for me. So, I became the proud owner of Eclipse Salon for 15 years, until it was time for me to move to the next phase of my life. How God intervened for me in the acquisition of Eclipse Salon was typically how He intervened for me in business situations. Since He showed me such favor in so many instances, you would think I would have figured out sooner that I could trust Him with everything concerning me. But no, I had to handle my personal affairs myself, and did I ever make a mess out of it!

IN THE MASTER'S HANDS

Everything related to my career has mostly been in the category of an Ephesians 3:20 blessing: exceedingly, abundantly, above all that I could ask for or dream of. Now, it could be said that Tracci's life turned out just as she wanted it to. As far as my career, yes, I think it did, but there was never a time when my career was enough to chase away the emptiness and self-loathing I struggled with.

My career success didn't keep me from feeling alone and vulnerable. I lived with the stress that at any minute, I would not be able to maintain my charade of having it all together. There were times I struggled to the point of having suicidal thoughts. Some days it was a real task just to get up and get going because I was so tired of pretending. Even though God saw my inward struggles, insecurities, inadequacies, pain, and the tears I cried in the late-night hours, help was not available to me until I let go of my self-sufficiency and asked.

Ye have not, because ye ask not. (James 4:2)

RELYING ON HIS LOVE

I suffered intense internal turmoil because my view of God, the Father, was mingled with the attributes I saw in my earthly father. I had trouble relating to a God who loves me unconditionally. I couldn't grasp that I didn't have to earn His love or prove I was worthy of it. I just needed to accept the love He had already demonstrated when Jesus died to purchase my freedom from sin and death. The quality of my spiritual life didn't begin to change until I got it in my spirit that God's love for me is not performance-based. It revolutionized my thinking about myself, my sense of security, and my ability to trust God in all areas of my life. I would be lying if I said I never need to remind myself of who I am in Christ. But knowing and relying on God's love gives me the power to resist Satan's accusations and the assurance I am always welcomed in my Father's presence.

God's love for me is not performance-based.

A few years back, gospel singer/writer J. Moss recorded a song entitled "Good and Bad ". The song is an expression of appreciation for God's unconditional love and for His mercy that does not cancel out our future because of the sins of our past. To this sentiment, I say, "Praise God!" What's love got to do with it? God's love is security for those who are in Christ. That security is offered to anyone who will receive His finished work on the cross. What we choose to do with God's love, answers the question, "What's love got to do with it?" How we respond to His love will influence the quality of our lives in the present and determine where we spend eternity.

Have you fully embraced God's love for you? Or are you having trouble grasping the fact He loves you just because you are you? If you have trouble, identify past events that contribute to your inability to fully embrace the fact you are special to the Father. Pray for healing, and prayerfully seek Christian counseling, knowing God wants you healed and whole so He can get the glory in your life.

OUTWARD APPLICATION

Get together with some friends and plan ongoing *visits* to a rest home that houses the disabled or elderly. Some of them house disabled children exclusively. Take some small gifts: socks, caps, throws, lotions, books, etc. (Check with the facility for acceptable gifts.)

The goal is to show love and kindness—and if the opportunity presents itself, to share the gospel. For you who sing, rest homes are usually open to groups singing to patients, particularly during the Christmas holidays.

PRAYER

Dear Father, please help me accept that I matter to You because You love me individually, not just as a part of a collective group. Lord, please open doors for me to showcase Your love to people who may not be able to get to a church. In Jesus' name, I pray. Amen.

If you are not a Christian, or if you are not sure of your salvation, please refer to Chapter 10, "The Invitation". God loves you and wants you to be a part of His family for eternity.

Chapter 5

DON'T WORRY. BE HAPPY

"Our present troubles are small and won't last very long. Yet they produce for us a glory that vastly outweighs them and will last forever!"

(2 Corinthians 4:17 NLT)

Many years ago, Bobby McFerrin, Bob Marley, and other artists recorded a popular song, "Don't Worry. Be Happy". This song encourages us to make a conscious effort to choose happiness over worrying. Because there is usually a direct correlation between happiness and happenings, the reasons for happiness are fluid and evasive. "I'll be happy when I get married. I'll be happy when this divorce is over. I'll be happy when I have babies. I'll be happy when these kids are out of this house. I'll be happy when I get this dream job. I'll be happy when I can retire."

Exactly what does, "I'll be happy when…" mean anyway? Does it mean you'll be miserably unhappy until then? Does it mean nothing else can be substituted for your perceived happy thing? Is there any type of guarantee on your perceived happy thing? What if it doesn't live up to your expectations? Obviously, the bottom can drop out of happiness with one phone call, one piece of mail, or one event.

We seek happiness in such things as material gains, people, feel-good activities, various addictions, recognition, and ever-increasing status, but nothing in this world has any lasting value. There were times when I erroneously charged God with the task of making me happy, and if He failed to do the job I assigned to Him, I felt as if He let me down. Why? I believed that personally and individually, I didn't really matter to Him. Therefore, my feelings didn't matter to Him. It's a sad state to be in. The devil can leave you twisting in the wind when you buy into this lie.

THE PURSUIT OF HAPPINESS

For years, I got caught up in the pursuit of happiness. I replaced fulfilling my primary purpose, which is to glorify God, with my frantic search. And, I had tunnel vision about what constituted happiness—a husband and two babies. In the busyness of my pursuit, I didn't take the time to really think beyond the temporal, to meditate on heavenly issues, to take inventory of where my life was heading, or to seek guidance from the Lord. In retrospect, the problem was when I slowed down, I could hear the muffled cries of the wounded child inside of me. I had to suppress her so I could continue to function as the strong, self-sufficient, take-charge woman I was driven to represent in the world. I couldn't slow down and let my thoughts catch up with me because in the stillness of my thoughts, there was a deafening reality of just how unhappy and discontented I was with life.

> We get caught up in doing good things rather than God things.

Busyness is one of Satan's most effective tactics because it distracts us from the things of God, as we get caught up in doing good things rather than God things. Early in my career, I got a lot of exposure in the industry. I had a wonderful publicist who really got my name out there. My salon was one of the hottest salons on the African American hair circuit and in addition to some clients in the entertainment industry, we serviced several professional basketball players and their wives. Besides celebrity tours, I was on television make-over shows, styled on television movie sets, and did photo and video shoots. Several trade magazines and a couple of other magazines featured me, and/or my salon. I even landed on the cover of a couple. My life was non-stop busyness, and there was little time for reflection on its meaningfulness.

While still in my twenties, I had everything I could want materially because of my success in the industry. But it was never enough to make me happy. I lived in an apartment complex where several television and movie celebrities lived. It was a fabulous, very exclusive complex. There were pools, on-sight-dry-cleaners, a library, a gym, and a concierge. You couldn't even apply to live in the complex unless a present tenant wrote a referral for you. I was living in my dream apartment full of my dream furnishings. With my interior design skills and the collaboration of a friend, my apartment looked like it should have been in some interior design magazine—no, on the cover.

BUT JUST SAD

I was highly successful, making lots of money, capable of buying whatever I wanted, driving a Mercedes convertible, and wearing the top fashions—but just sad! Anyone looking from the outside would think I was living the good life, full of everything that would make anyone happy. But I was miserable down to the core of my soul!

I didn't know anyone that I could be transparent with. I didn't even want my mother to know that I was a success in business but a failure in life. I was always pretending—to be happy—to be grounded—to be in charge. I kept buying things to make me feel better, but nothing worked. I was never reckless with my money because I valued my good credit, but I did spend a lot of it unnecessarily. Then as time passed, I turned to food. Now, that was the beginning of a downward spiral of enormous proportion because I could also afford to eat whatever, wherever, and whenever I wanted. I started gaining weight, and for someone whose worth was wrapped up in her image, that was disastrous! I felt very unattractive as I was forced to buy larger clothes. Soon, my closet contained about four different sizes as my weight fluctuated. This made me feel even more desperate because I really wanted to get married. And now, I was losing control of what I thought I needed to find this man—my looks!

I was a success in business but a failure in life.

Then one day, the proverbial straw that broke the camel's back presented itself. Because I was often in magazines, I got calls from stylists across the nation wanting to work with me. Many of them wanted to connect with me so they could connect to the lifestyle they envisioned for themselves. Some stylists came to work at my salon with the expectations of reaching my level of success and were disappointed when it didn't happen overnight. Some became jealous and created a hostile environment in the salon. They'd take every opportunity to make snide remarks and made it obvious their hostility was directed towards me. This scenario was very disturbing to me because I took pride in the camaraderie in the salon.

A NAGGING FEELING

Before I could deal with the problems I already had at the salon, I made a big mistake that made things worst. I got a call from a young woman from Oakland. I didn't know her well when I lived in Oakland, but she told me that she had admired me and wanted desperately to work with me to develop her skills. Maybe it was because I needed a new friendly face in the salon, or perhaps I remembered how difficult it was for me to get started in Los Angeles, but I agreed for her to come. In the back of my mind, I had a nagging feeling that I had heard her name associated with something negative, but I couldn't remember what it was. I should have made some calls to check her out, but I didn't. I just let her come.

To help this new stylist succeed, I gave her the new clients who called for appointments with me. And when I had to go out of town for a series of workshops, I let her service my clients, including some of my celebrity clients. When I returned after one of my trips, I noticed the atmosphere in the salon seemed more toxic than usual. Then strange things started to happen. Some of my clients walked into the salon without speaking to me and walked straight to this new stylist's station. I found out she was telling people we hung out together in Oakland, to give credibility to the lies she obviously told about me. She was trying to ruin my reputation and my business—the two things that meant the most to me. I don't know why she thought destroying me was going to help her. I was stabbed in the back by her but what hurt the most was some of my long-term clients chose to believe her and not bother to fact-check. This stylist left the salon, opened her own salon, and took some of my clients, but her business only lasted a short time before it failed. The last information I got about her was that she had a mental breakdown. Maybe that explains her actions.

THE SUM OF MY WORTH

When I arrived home that night after discovering what this stylist had done, I was at the lowest point of my life. The atmosphere in my salon was tense and toxic, and I didn't know how to fix it, or how not to let it bother me. I didn't know who I could trust. I didn't know who was

talking behind my back because of something this person said. I didn't
even know what she said or who she said it to. And I didn't know what
to do about any of it. How do you fight against lies when some people
have their own motives for believing the worst? I felt like everyone
was smiling in my face but stabbing
me in my back. My reputation—how
people saw me—was the sum of my
worth, but now it was tainted!

**Satan thought
He had me that
night... But God!**

Lying on my face before God in the
middle of my living room floor, I tried
to come to grips with what I was feeling—my world was caving in on me.
I was in the darkest of dark places. The thought that I am who God
says I am never entered my mind. That was not a part of my thought
pattern yet. I was sick in the pit of my stomach, and for the first time
since my friend, Ron Newton, committed suicide, I really understood
how a person with seemingly everything to live for could take his
life. There I was struggling to find a reason and the strength to make
it through the night. Nothing I owned, none of the accolades, and
nothing I had accomplished gave any meaning to my life. Everything
was worthless and life was hopeless. There was no happiness to be
found anywhere or in anything. To this day, I know Satan thought he
had me that night, and I am not convinced that he didn't. But God!

I searched my mind for anyone I could call, but I cringed when I
thought about the last time I got the nerves to confide in someone.
I confided in her just wanting her to walk with me through my darkness,
but she brushed me off with this attitude: "How dare you complain!
Look at all the people around you who wish they were in your shoes!
Get over it!" The reason I confided in her in the first place was that
she asked me how I was doing. But most people really don't want to
hear anything but, "I'm fine." They don't want to hear life is crushing

in on you. I get it! Most people are plagued with their own problems, and they don't want to or cannot support you in yours, especially if how you look doesn't give credibility to your problems.

I don't know how to explain the mental, emotional, and spiritual agony I suffered that night as I kept going over and over the events of the day. My salon that I had worked so hard for, was no longer a safe place for me. For the first time since I was saved at 8 years old, I truly realized that I had nowhere to turn but to God. I was boxed in on all sides. I could no longer shoulder my own burdens. All my strength was gone. I cried out to God that night as I had never done before! I needed Him to show me who He really is, and I needed it then! At that point, I couldn't see how I would make it through the night. I begged God for a friend, not a boyfriend, just a real friend—someone who wouldn't be scared away if I confided my darkest feelings, someone who would not use my pain against me, and someone who would not pull away when I revealed just how troubled my heart was.

> **My salon was no longer a safe place for me.**

MY ANGEL FRIEND

I felt as if my prayers were falling on deaf ears. After all, I had been living my life like I was in charge for years. I had taken pride in my self-sufficiency—being able to take care of myself and solve my own problems. As I surveyed my situation that night, God showed me the futility of self-sufficiency as He stripped it away from me. I saw just how much I had dishonored Him. So why was He going to listen now? As I sank deeper into a black hole of despair sensing I was going down for the count, my phone rang! On the other end was an angel! God sent me an angel! It was my long-lost friend, Pennae!

When I was traveling with the styling team representing the state of California, I was paired together in the hotels with a very beautiful, very funny young woman who was also on the styling team representing the state of Pennsylvania. She was a few years older than me and had been a stylist longer, but we really clicked. Pennae and I were very different, although I discovered early on that she was also a Christian. It seemed that she was much more carnal than I was because her flaws were more visible than mine. She was loud, flashy, and used profanity often. The words just rolled off her tongue. She was, for lack

Me and Pennae, the year we met when we were on the International styling team.

of a better phrase, rough around the edges, and made no apologies for who she was. I wasn't used to Christians using profanity with such ease. On the other hand, I was always on my best behavior. I cared so much about what people thought of me. I always wanted to look good on the outside—like I had it all together professionally, emotionally, and spiritually. Neither was true. Pennae and I were both struggling with carnality but just in very different ways.

Despite our differences, there was something about Pennae that drew me to her. She was unique—like no one I had known before. She was very complimentary of my skills, and sincerely encouraged me when she sensed I was fighting any insecurities. Even with my skills, insecurity was always lurking in the shadows. What was particularly refreshing was I never felt any undercurrent of competition or comparison between us—no cattiness. She was very comfortable doing *her* while encouraging me to do *me* at the highest level possible. I admired her confidence, her free spirit, and her styling skills. She was not bound by what people thought of her, or a need for validation from those she encountered. After our travels with the team, we both moved on. Eventually, I lost contact with my friend. I once tried to find her in Pennsylvania but with no success. I didn't know that she had relocated to Atlanta.

HELLO BEAUTIFUL

That pivotal night, the first words out of Pennae's mouth were, "Hello, Beautiful, I've been looking for you forever." She told me how God put it on her heart to reach out to me because He showed her although I was very successful in my career, I was very sad. Her words hit a nerve, and the flimsy curtain that separated my public image from my tortured soul vanished. I started bawling—deep heaving sobs like a dam broke inside of me. There was such a release in my spirit, I knew at that moment that God had not only heard me, but was answering my prayers. He sent me a lifeline named Pennae.

Almost immediately, I notice that Pennae was different. She had grown spiritually and even though she was still loud, and still funny, it was apparent she'd had an encounter with God that had ushered her into her prophetic gift and the gift of intercessory prayer. That night, she spoke into my life as no one had ever done before or since. She listened to the ugliness of where I was without trying to convince me I had no right to my feelings. She encouraged me without shaming me for not being happy with all my "stuff." When people are depressed, giving them reasons why they shouldn't be is not a good approach, especially when the encourager erroneously thinks anything in this world can satisfy the longings of the soul.

Pennae allowed me to own my pain, met me where I was, and prayed for me until I felt my burdens lift. I join the Psalmist in his declaration.

> My suffering was good for me, for it taught me to pay attention to your decrees. Your instructions are more valuable to me than millions in gold and silver.
> (Psalm 119:71-72 NLT)

I thank God for every difficult lesson He orchestrated to teach me that I can't make it without Him. Since that night, Pennae has proven repeatedly that she is the tailor-made friend God prepared for me. She wants nothing or needs nothing but to be my friend. She is the most unselfish person I know, and I know that's saying a lot. Still, I mean every word.

In the years after this reunion with Pennae, I did a lot of traveling for trade shows—lecturing and doing demonstration workshops. There were times when Pennae and the entire staff from her salon in Atlanta would travel to meet me in whatever state an event was being held. I never asked them, but they would pay their own expenses to come to support me. They never accepted any money in return. They were just there for me. Whether they collected tickets, gave out programs, set up for demonstrations, organized and participated in product sales, interacted with the audience, or whatever was needed, they were there. Then when I did workshops in Atlanta, Pennae arranged for her salon to be available as my headquarters. It is one thing for Pennae to love me enough to support me at her expense, but it really shows the type of person she is when her staff loved her enough to support her in supporting me.

Me and Pennae just a couple of years ago.

My relationship with Pennae has developed into one of mutual support and transparency. We can deliver hard messages of correction to each other, even argue, and still reaffirm our love for each other in the same conversation. I am eternally grateful for my *angel* friend. Since that pivotal night, I've been blessed over the years with many wonderful friends whom I dearly love. God gave me exceedingly, abundantly above what I asked for when I asked for a friend. And I have reconnected with some of my friends who have been an important part of my life from my youth. These women have supported me through prayer and encouragement over a lifetime. I value each one of them because their support has been unwavering. Because of all the wonderful friends God has blessed me with, I am committed to being a true friend and encourager to the people I encounter because I know the value of true friendship.

THE STRUGGLE IS REAL

I wish I could say God instantaneously delivered me from my twisted thinking, but that's not true. Sometimes God does deliver quickly, but my deliverance was a process, a long, drawn-out struggle, which began that fateful night when my angel friend, Pennae called me. I will admit that I got discouraged when some of my issues continued to linger in my heart. I used to think my struggling was a sign of weakness, but I now know, that's not true. It was a sign of my resolve not to quit. Somewhere I heard winners never quit, and quitters never win. Struggling was my commitment to no longer let Satan walk all over me. And it also indicated my willingness to do the work to replace my flawed perceptions with the truth, as I am drawing closer to the Lord. Struggling assures me beyond a shadow of a doubt, God has something better for me, and something better in me, and He won't let me quit. The strength and security I have now did not come from always getting it right, or by a swoop of God's hand, but by pressing on and learning from my mistakes.

Unresolved issues would not go away just because I tried to ignore them or drown them out. Anything I used to eradicate them was only a band-aid, a cheap one at that. Reflection time, no matter how painful, is very important for our mental, emotional, and spiritual health. When I couldn't run from me anymore, I had to slow down and ask the Holy Spirit to dredge up all those wounds and heal them. And during the process, I had to stand in my pain—to cry, and sometimes wail because I knew that I had tried everything else, and God was my only hope.

Our commitment to God cannot be happiness-based.

Happiness is a blessing from God, and most of us are blessed with people, events, and opportunities that bring us happiness. Even though happiness can be a by-product of a well-spent life, still our commitment to God cannot be happiness-based. When we make the decision to follow Christ, there is no guaranteed happiness clause. We must be willing to be inconvenienced and sacrificial in our service to the Lord. In Christ, we can find joy and peace that are not dependent on happenings. To accept a relationship with God through the sacrifice of His Son, Jesus Christ, is the most important decision in life, and the only pursuit that offers eternal security.

INWARD APPLICATION

Examine your heart. Are you satisfied with your relationship with the Lord? Are you satisfied with your commitment to the Kingdom? Why or why not? What are you going to do about it if you are not satisfied?

OUTWARD APPLICATION

Prayerfully seek professional Christian counseling if you've had an ongoing struggle emotionally, mentally, or spiritually. A Christian counselor can point you in the direction of self-awareness and help you unearth the origin of your problems. Counseling can reveal to you that you are not the only one with a particular set of problems. This will help you in your prayer life as you seek God for spiritual and emotional healing. Some churches offer reasonable counseling services, but if not, counseling is well worth the expense. Don't continue to be trapped in events from your past. Get up and fight!

> Finally, my brethren, be strong in the Lord, and in the power of his might. Put on the whole armor of God, that ye may be able to stand against the wiles of the devil.
>
> (Ephesians 6:10)

Read all of Chapter 6. You won't be fighting your fight alone! God has already given you the tools needed to win. Fight the good fight! With the Lord, you will win!

PRAYER

Lord, please re-focus my life. Help me to submit to You completely. No matter the sacrifice, let my life count for the Kingdom in these last days. Let the work I do not be done in vain. Lord, please help me to allow You to shine Your light on every dark place in my heart, and then let me allow You to heal me. In Jesus' name, I pray. Amen.

If you are not a Christian or if you are not sure of your salvation, please refer to Chapter 10, "The Invitation". God loves you and He wants to heal you as only He can.

Chapter 6

SURRENDER

"For the grace of God has appeared bringing salvation for all people, instructing us to deny all godlessness and worldly lusts and to live in a sensible, righteous, and godly way in the present age, while we wait for the blessed hope, the appearing of the glory of our great God and Savior, Jesus Christ."

(Titus 2:11-12 CSB)

An old hymn of the church says, "All to Jesus, I surrender. All to Him I freely give. I will ever love and trust Him, in His presence daily live. I surrender all. I surrender all. All to Thee my blessed Savior, I surrender all." The words of this song eloquently express the sentiments of something I heard some church mothers say when I was a child, although not as eloquently, "Just let go and let God." It sounds simple enough, but surrendering your all to Jesus, is easier said than done. Surrendering is not a one-time event, and some areas of our lives are easier to surrender than others. Being saved and being surrendered are not synonymous. I accepted Jesus as my Savior when I was a child but still struggled for years to surrender to His Lordship.

It is natural for us to make plans for our lives, and making plans is biblical. It allows us to identify key components necessary to fulfill our plans and avoid possible hindrances.

> For which of you, desiring to build a tower, does not first sit down and count the cost, whether he has enough to complete it? (Luke 14:28 ESV)

While planning is biblical, planning independently of God is not. Scripture teaches us we can plan the course of our lives, but it is the Lord who directs our steps.

> A man's mind plans his way [as he journeys through life].
> But the Lord directs his steps and establishes them.
> (Proverbs 16:9 AMP)

The process of learning the importance of surrendering to God in all areas of my life was a tedious one. A vague knowledge of God does not provide the power, conviction, or trust necessary to reach the point of surrender, especially when the stakes are high. It wasn't until I embraced the God of the Bible—God's self-revelations of who He is, that I was able to denounce the many flawed perceptions I had about Him, which were greatly hindering my spiritual growth and effectiveness in the Kingdom.

ROAD TO SURRENDER

As a child, I learned the lessons taught in Sunday school and from Bible storybooks, and I wanted to be obedient to the Lord. I didn't realize it at the time, but my view of God's love for me was performance-based. I believed He loved me only when I saw myself as a good girl, so I wanted to be good so He would love me. It was very much like my approach to my earthly father. I wanted to show him I was worthy of his love, but I grew up never achieving my goal. Nevertheless, through Christ, I am now okay with that.

My view of God's love for me was performance-based.

In my early teenage years, God started challenging me more in the areas of my thoughts, my motivations, and the false truths I was developing—the kinds of things only God can see. I was really lacking in those areas. Even then, the hand of God was determining my steps, sometimes directing me with a still, small voice or a gentle tug at my heart. Those were the times when I was in tune with Him and waiting with expectation to hear from Him. But there were far too many times when I anticipated God giving me directions I didn't want to surrender to, so I developed a bad habit of acting like I was hard of hearing, as if God didn't know my thoughts even before I formed them in my mind.

I've heard people talk about unique ways God gets their attention or guides them—ways other than what they read in the Bible. If we are in tune with the Holy Spirit, He may speak to us through a strong impression or maybe we can feel what He is saying in our spirits, even when we don't hear an audible sound. Just in case the devil tries to counterfeit a message, we do need to understand that God's messages will never contradict His written Word. Sometimes, the Holy Spirit redirects me through a very selective upset stomach. I say selective because it only bothered me under select circumstances. It's like a stomach alarm. Sometimes I ignored these promptings, but it always proved to be a bad idea. This time when I tried to ignore my stomach alarm, I had an extraordinary experience. It was what I call a *forced surrender* situation.

I've had my share of forced surrenders. Usually, they occurred after I had run out of options and had no other choices. It's amazing to me how God can focus on the details of my life as though He has nothing else to do. This time when I was forced to surrender, it drastically changed my life because God revealed Himself to me in a way that revolutionized my relationship with Him. It was my *Red Sea* experience. And it was the last time I purposely ignored His efforts to get my attention when it came to my career.

DO YOU HEAR ME NOW?

I was well on my way to fulfilling my plans that would assure my success as a celebrity hairstylist. You might say I was destined to be a hairstylist. My paternal grandmother told me that her great-grand-mother worked making wigs with Madam C.J. Walker, the first African American woman millionaire. The story is that my paternal aunt was one of, if not the first African American to own a salon in Beverly Hills. She was also a celebrity hairstylist who traveled the country with a renowned hairstyling team called the "Trendsetters." My maternal grandmother was a hairstylist and salon owner, as were two of her sisters. Another sister was a barber and shop owner. She was known as the best barber in town and a pioneer in becoming a female shop owner in the state of Texas. Later, she owned a shop in Oakland, California. So, I have a rich heritage of beauty professionals, and I had big plans to make my mark in the beauty industry.

To fulfill my dreams, I knew it would take serious discipline, hard work, and determination. But even at a young age, I understood the importance of putting God first as I pursued my dreams. However, I was selective in which areas of my life I put God first. My heart was set on working at a particular salon after finishing school. It was the top salon in Oakland, California at that time—Center Stage West. The star stylist was Ron Newton, son of Black Panther leader Huey P. Newton, and I wanted to be mentored by him. But the problem was, I had never met him and didn't know anyone who knew him. In my prayers, I shared with God my dream of working with Ron, and I believed somehow it would happen. I'm not trying to sound super-spiritual, but at that point, I really did believe it.

One day, when I was at the beauty school, God began His definitive pattern of showing me favor in my career. Ron Newton came to the school looking for an assistant. He asked the instructor who was the most talented student at the school, and she pointed me out. When she approached me with the news of her recommendation, I knew God was answering my prayers. I clearly understood He had orchestrated the events that were opening career doors.

Ron Newton not only became my mentor and teacher, but he also became my best friend. I worked under him for a year as a student, then I became a peer and co-worker. I was the only female stylist in an all-male environment. I quickly became one of the most sought-out stylists in Oakland and the surrounding cities. While still in Oakland, I worked with a few celebrity clients, even going on a tour with one. These experiences gave me a taste of where my career could go and reinforced my desire to be a hairstylist in the entertainment industry.

Since my goal was to become a celebrity stylist, I believed Los Angeles offered me greater opportunities, so I prayed for guidance until I was confident God was releasing me to make the move. You may wonder why I wanted a clientele that included people in the entertainment industry. Well, it was not because I was star-struck. Even as a teenager, I was never a "groupie." You wouldn't find me at a concert yelling until I lost my voice or passing out with excitement. But I envisioned a career styling the hair of people who needed a polished look in their line of work and who could afford to pay the prices I charged for my signature look. Also, the variety of opportunities the entertainment industry offers that go beyond standing in a salon all day appealed to me. Once in Los Angeles, I found many women who were not in the entertainment industry but were also willing to pay for my signature look. Often, my clients get inquiries about who does their hair. When they respond, they get, "I knew that looked like Tracci's work."

On moving day, I packed up and moved to Los Angeles to start this new chapter in my life. Everyone I talked to thought I was crazy for leaving such a lucrative clientele, but I kept my focus on my goal. I had an assurance in my spirit that God was directing my career, and He had already shown Himself faithful in my career goals. Although I must admit, I found it much easier to trust God with my career than my personal life. After I paid off all my bills, I left for Los Angeles with $10,000 in hand. I would have had much more money if I hadn't been such a fan of clothes. Still, I was confident that $10,000 would sustain me until I built a clientele in Los Angeles. However, it didn't take long for that money to dry up because my plans for my housing situation fell through almost immediately. I made plans to live with my father until I got established, although I hadn't lived with him since age one. Big mistake! He made living with him impossible, so I moved out shortly after I moved in.

NO SUPPORT SYSTEM

I found myself with no support system because I didn't want anyone to know what was going on with me. Did you notice that I said I found myself with no support system? What happened to the God who had been faithful in directing my career? Where was the God who showed me professional favor? Did I only trust Him when I could see my own way clear? Could I only trust Him in low-stakes situations? Is trust only trust until it is tested?

I was homeless for a period. I slept in my car, in hotel lobbies, or sometimes I'd scrape up enough money for a cheap motel. Finally,

I swallowed my pride and confided in a few of my clients about my situation. Some clients let me sleep on their sofa for a night or two. The last time I stayed at a client's house, there was a domestic violence incident that took place when the boyfriend came over. After that, I didn't have the appetite for staying in strange houses.

As worry set in, panic totally replaced praying. That fact alone demonstrated a serious lack of trust in God. The Apostle Paul admonished the Philippian church with these words:

> **As worry set in, panic totally replaced praying.**

> Do not be anxious about anything, but in every situation, by prayer and petition, with thanksgiving, present your requests to God. (Philippians 4:6)

It wasn't that I didn't know this scripture was in the Bible, but the scripture wasn't in me. As fear gripped me, during one of my sleepless nights, I came up with what I thought was a brilliant plan. Since I had such an extensive clientele in Oakland, I would travel from Los Angeles to Oakland and work there for the first two or three days of the week, then return to Los Angeles to work for the remainder of the week. My Oakland clients were happy with this new arrangement. This plan provided me with enough money to live since I could not survive with the meager clientele I had in Los Angeles. With a big sigh of relief, I patted myself on the back because I had solved my problem myself, and now I could relax and go back to trusting God for the less important problems.

During that time, Greyhound bus tickets were a lot cheaper and the bus much more convenient than the airlines because the Oakland bus station was located near where I needed to be. However, I truly hated even walking into the bus station. The sidewalk outside and the floor inside were always extremely dirty, and there was always that distinct smell of urine. I felt like I wanted to throw my shoes in the garbage each time I walked in all that filth.

I hated being on the bus even more than I hated the filthy bus station. I always left late on a Sunday night, and there were always some scary-looking people on the bus. This was unsettling, to say the least. Still, I soon became aware God was showing me favor delivered through the bus drivers. I encountered many different bus drivers of various races, but every time I got on the bus, the driver would offer me the seat directly to the right of him. No one was ever in that seat when I got on the bus, and no one ever sat next to me. Different buses on different nights, with different drivers, but I was always offered the same seat. Of course, being next to the driver, and not having to share my seat provided a level of comfort that allowed me to stretch out and go to sleep.

THE STOMACH ALARM

From the first day in Oakland, I was booked solid. I only needed to work two days a week because I scheduled 30 clients a day. I was making thousands of dollars in two days. Although I was making much-needed money and I felt God's protection over me, in my spirit, I felt God wasn't pleased with my plan to go back and forth to Oakland. I had this sense God was saying, I released you to go to Los Angeles, and you need to trust Me to sustain you. Then I noticed, starting with the third trip I made to Oakland, my stomach alarm was activated. From then on, every week as I got on the bus, I had this sick feeling in the pit of my stomach that seemed to get worse each week; yet, miraculously, it didn't bother me at any other time during the week. It was not the first time discomfort in my stomach served as a warning that God was redirecting me. This was a familiar pattern by this time, and I didn't doubt what God was saying to me, but I was trying to ignore Him. I was too afraid to give up on my plan—to give up control and trust Him to sustain me. I was afraid to let go and let God because that required a level of trust I had not yet learned to operate in.

So, even with my stomach alarm going off each Sunday night, I kept going to Oakland. I got a small apartment and a little furniture in Los Angeles, and I started servicing my Los Angeles clients at my apartment because I could save money by not paying both apartment rent and booth rent at a salon. And I still had my expenses for my trips to Oakland. If I couldn't pay for my apartment, then I'd have no place to work or to live in Los Angeles. So, I reasoned that I needed to continue going to Oakland until I felt comfortable with the amount of money I was making in Los Angeles, and I was a long way from being comfortable. I assured God I would stop traveling to Oakland as soon as I could. What I really meant was as soon as I felt secure with what I could accomplish on my own. The fact that I was bargaining with God on the subject shows I really did know what He wanted me to do. Nothing in my thoughts or in my actions indicated I was trusting God because I wasn't. I was trusting in myself, and I had reduced God to a good luck charm, just there to support my plans. By now, my stomach discomfort was getting worse—a strong apprehension, like a foreboding of doom, and the epic center of the discomfort was in the pit of my stomach, which caused a loss of appetite. Although, that part wasn't all bad.

I wouldn't even entertain the thought of doing what I knew God was saying to me. So, after several weeks, God performed a miracle, but not in the sense that we usually think of miracles. In fact, it was a miracle of biblical proportions. As I said before, I averaged 30 clients a day when I worked in Oakland. I had an assistant who did the shampooing, conditioning, and coloring for me. Her help made it possible for me to complete so many clients in the allotted time. We had to work late into the night to get all the clients done, but they didn't complain. They were just happy I was there. Also, we worked on days the salon would normally be closed so the only clients in the salon were mine. So, we had plenty of space to work.

WHAT?

The week before my last week in Oakland, I did 60 clients in two days—everyone showed up on time. I was fully booked again on what turned out to be my last week in Oakland. I had 60 scheduled and confirmed appointments over a period of two days. Every appointment slot was filled. I had already counted how much money I would make and made written plans for how I would spend the money. But do you know that not one customer showed up or called that first day! Not one! I was in a state of shock because I had never had a problem with no-shows. In fact, it is almost unheard of in my salon for clients not to show or fail to reschedule in advance. It just doesn't happen.

> **I had this inkling that God was somehow involved.**

I sat there dumbfounded as client after client failed to show for their appointments. I turned ideas over and over in my mind seeking an explanation for this phenomenon. Was I looking on the wrong page in the appointment book, or did I say the wrong date? Did the clients think they were scheduled for the following week? Did someone get my client list and call my clients to cancel their appointments for some vindictive reason? I couldn't sort out all my different emotions. I was scared, confused, amazed, bewildered, shocked, embarrassed, and a host of other emotions because this situation made no sense. Any explanation I came up with didn't fit the circumstances. Somewhere in the back of my mind, I had this inkling that God was somehow involved. But I kept rejecting that idea because that would mean I was dealing with a God so much bigger than I could wrap my mind around! It wasn't that I didn't believe God spoke the world into existence, parted the Red Sea, or formed man from the dust of the ground, but those events were during biblical times. Those were special events for special people, but this was a situation involving me.

I just sat there in a stupor waiting from early morning to late that night—no shows—not one! I wonder what the odds are of something like that happening—astronomical; I'm sure. After a while, I just stopped talking to my assistant about the repeated no-shows and sat quietly in expectation that no one was coming. I was trying to reconcile in my mind that the God of the universe would stage such a dramatic display of His power. What was the purpose? Why would He allow this situation to happen to me? He knew how hard I was working to get on my feet. He knew that I was a faithful tither and according to Malachi Chapter 3, God should have been pouring me out blessings that I could not contain. What happened to that promise? I didn't sleep all night rehearsing the events of the day.

If I hadn't figured out that it was God's doing by the end of the first day, I sure knew by the beginning of the second day. It was a repeat performance of the day before. I was almost in a catatonic state from the events of the first day, but now it was worse! I felt like I was in "The Twilight Zone", from an old weekly television show I watched as a teenager. In the series, people experienced strange, sometimes, out-of-body experiences as they were caught in a twilight zone. If ever there was a miracle in my life, that was it! It was as though God came down from Heaven to get in my face and say, "Do you understand the words that are coming out of My mouth? Do not go back to Oakland to work! Period! End of story!"

You may be thinking is she for real? Did that really happen? Is she making this up to impress us? Just let me say impressing you is not important enough to jeopardize God's blessings in my life. I want the best God has for me, and I want to glorify Him with my life. Yes, it did really happen—just like I'm telling it! My assistant and I were both there. When I told my mother about those life-changing two days, she kept asking questions and having me repeat certain parts of the story, not because she didn't believe me but because she was trying to wrap her mind around it too. I call this experience one of forced surrender. God closed every door to every self-help plan I had, but He didn't do it just to discipline me for my disobedience. He did it to teach me that my perception of Him was much too small and full of errors. He did it to put me in a position where I had no choice but to trust Him and in doing so, I learned that He is, indeed, trustworthy.

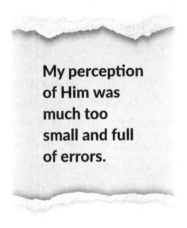

My perception of Him was much too small and full of errors.

A SET UP FOR A COMEBACK

But wait! You need to hear the second part of the miracle! There was absolutely nothing left for me to do but surrender and cling to God for dear life. I was so shocked that I couldn't even think of anything else to do. I was just beaten down. God had me boxed in, but in His loving grace, He was setting me up for a miraculous comeback. Sometimes we need to be put in situations where all we can do is stand still and see the salvation of the Lord.

I limped my troubled soul back to Los Angeles knowing I would never return to Oakland to work. I cried most of the way back home. All I could think about was I did not have the money necessary to sustain me. I couldn't even pray in faith because I didn't expect God to help me anyway. I had, once again, ignored His directions when I fully understood them. He wanted me to choose to trust Him, but I wouldn't even entertain the thought. Too much was at stake. I knew I deserved to be punished and God was justified in doing so. And even if He wanted to, I didn't see any way He could possibly help me in time to avoid financial ruin. Oh, I surrendered alright! There was nothing left to do. Not only did I surrender, but with a stiff upper lip, I braced myself for the inevitable—financial ruin. And with a sense of nobility, I decided I had to be okay with that, even if I was destined to sleep in my car again.

Thank God, He does not always deal with me according to what I deserve! Sometimes He just looks past my faults and sees my needs. God knew I wanted to trust Him, but I hadn't learned how. I can imagine Him saying, "Come on, daughter, let me show you great and wonderful things." Considering the irrefutable truth God revealed to me, over time, I let go of flawed perceptions and learned the truth about who He is and who I am as His daughter. Not only did He teach me He is enough all by Himself, but He also taught me I am enough for Him to love with unconditional love.

The first week back from Oakland, God performed part two of His miracle! I went from very few clients in Los Angeles to being booked solid. My appointment book looked like it did in Oakland, and from then on, I had plenty of clients! God showed me just as He dried up my clients in Oakland, He could open the floodgates in Los Angeles. I don't know where all those people came from! I never lacked clients from that day. Approximately two years later, God blessed me to purchase my dream (10 booths) salon that had an original asking price of over $200,000, for $10,000. Favor!

So, I can sing with the saints of old, "All to Jesus, I surrender. All to Him I freely give. I will ever love and trust Him. In His presence daily live. I surrender all. I surrender all. All to Thee my blessed Savior, I surrender all." He is the same yesterday, today, and forevermore!

INWARD APPLICATION

What areas in your life are you having trouble surrendering to God? Spend quiet time with God and ask Him to reveal what those areas are and why you haven't been able to surrender them. Then confess and ask for the help from the Holy Spirit living in you.

OUTWARD APPLICATION

Many Christians fall short in obeying God's Great Commission to go and share the gospel. Evangelism is neglected in the church. Purpose in your heart that you won't be one who neglects it. Find a class or some good books to sharpen your skills, then get with a group in the church to obey the mandate to go. Purpose in your heart to surrender to God in this area.

PRAYER

Lord, help me develop a relationship of transparency with You. Teach me to lean and depend on You because You are trustworthy. In Jesus' name, I pray. Amen.

If you are not a Christian, or you are unsure of your salvation, please refer to Chapter 10, "The Invitation". God loves you and wants you to be a part of His family. He is waiting for you to come to Him.

Chapter 7

STRAIGHT AND NARROW

"Trust in the Lord with all your heart, and do not rely
on your own understanding; in all your ways know
Him, and He will make your paths straight."

(Proverbs 3:5-6 CSB)

The term "straight and narrow" is usually associated with proper conduct, and it could apply to how a Christian should live. In fact, God gives us a mandate that can keep us on the straight and narrow, if we follow it.

If you have read a couple of chapters in this book, you already know I was a slow learner when it came to staying on the straight and narrow. Real life changes don't happen just because we read scriptures printed on pages or even quote them from memory. Real life changes occur when we take the Author of the Scriptures at His Word, allow His Word to take root in our hearts, and commit to living by it in the power of the Holy Spirit. One of the great tragedies of my life was having the knowledge of what the Bible says while living in defeat because of lack of application.

MAZE LIVING

Typically, a maze is a puzzle that is solved using paper and pencil to find a path that will lead you out of the maze—to the finish line. In Yancheng, China, there is a sprawling permanent maze called Yancheng Dafeng Dream Maze, which is, according to the *Guinness Book of World Records*, the largest maze pathway in the world. It is a tourist site and people flock there to try their skills at navigating through this network of paths enclosed by hedges as tall as humans. This maze is designed to be a complicated puzzle with many choices of paths you can travel, multiple options of entrances and exits, lots of dead-ends, do-overs, retraced steps, before you finally discover the exit that frees you, if you do, in fact, find it.

While reading an article about this massive maze, I saw how a maze is a great analogy for a Christian going through life disconnected from God's guidance. In fact, I would suggest there is an even larger maze than the one in China. It is worldwide and individualized, and Satan is the mastermind behind it. It offers many choices of paths you can travel, and without God's guidance, you can waste your entire life. I will give this maze a name, "Maze of Futility." It is so treacherous it needs a big flashing red sign that says, "Beware of danger! Enter at your own risk!" This maze will negatively impact your witness, stifle your God-given purpose, deny you blessings and rewards, rob you of valuable time, and render your Christian life ineffective!

Without God's guidance, you can waste your entire life.

King Solomon, the wisest man who ever lived, had too much of everything. He didn't deny himself anything he desired or refuse himself any pleasure. Still, as his life was coming to an end, he concluded that pursuing life independently of God was like the pursuit of wind: futile and meaningless. Being your own tour guide through life won't get you to a desirable location, and it won't fulfill the longing inside. It won't keep you on the straight and narrow.

AN INFORMED DECISION

Our church had a movie night presentation from the 1970s entitled, "A Thief in the Night." It is like a forerunner of the "Left Behind" series, but it is more biblically sound in its presentation. I've cherished my old VHS copy of this movie for many years. Although they now have DVD copies, I still watch my old VHS copy from time to time, and I've shown it to others. There is a background song in different parts of the movie that has this haunting melody and the words, "You've been left behind." Something about those words got stuck in my spirit that night. I had been taught God's plan of salvation at home, so I understood what was going on in the movie, maybe more than the average eight-year-old child. When the invitation was given after the movie, I knew what I needed to do. I made an informed decision to receive Christ as my personal Savior. Lord knows I didn't want to be left behind!

Me and my brother, the day of my baptism.

My mother taught my brother and me at home, and she was our first Sunday school teacher. She would move up to teach the next age group as we advanced because she was adamant about us not being taught anything wrong, often referring to Biblical errors she was taught as a kid. My mother was saved only three years before I was born, and one of her spiritual gifts turned out to be teaching. She quickly developed into an awesome Bible teacher. I was in her Bible studies in many different settings as I grew up. Along with my church friends, I always wanted to be in her class during special workshops or Vacation Bible School. I even had several friends who tried to stay in my mother's Sunday school class after it was time for their promotion to the next level. My mother was also very hospitable. She enjoyed cooking and watching people eat her food, so my friends from church frequented our home. Many of them have kept in touch with her for the last 30-plus years.

When we bought our first house, it was in a quiet neighborhood in Oakland, California, that had many elderly homeowners. The neighborhood started to change as the elderly homeowners died, and their children, grandchildren, relatives, or unrelated renters began living in the homes. Eventually, our neighborhood became notorious for crime: prostitution, drugs, break-ins, drive-by shootings, and even daytime murders. In front of our house, we witnessed dead bodies on the sidewalk at least three times, pimps beating and stomping prostitutes, and one drive-by shooting that put baseball-size holes in three consecutive houses starting with the house next door to us. The shooters came around the corner on two wheels, and by the time they had straightened out and started shooting, they had passed our house, which is probably why it was spared. But God! Later that same year, one of my friends who often sat on my front porch with me on long summer nights was found dead in the trunk of his car. His long hair was cut off and stuffed in his mouth. During that same summer, another car came around the corner so fast it jumped the curb and totaled my mother's car before it entered the side of our neighbor's house. Our neighborhood really changed.

Many nights, we could hear the tap-tap-tap of the heels of prostitutes walking up and down the sidewalk in front of our house. Sometimes, we could hear them as they walked up and sat on our porch. I'm sure their feet were hurting. They would even service "johns" on the side of our house. We would look down from upstairs and see them until my mother caught on to what we were doing. Despite the dangers that surrounded us, God protected our goings and comings. We never had a burglar alarm, and our exterior back door was made of flimsy plywood. Though we were frequently out at night, out-of-town for days, or sometimes weeks at a time, no one ever broke into our house in almost ten years. That was nothing but God!

> **Despite the dangers, God protected our goings and comings.**

During that period, there were some documentaries made about the drug traffic in our neighborhood. One reporter from a local news station did a ride-along with the self-proclaimed "drug king" of our side of town. The interview was filmed from inside his candy-apple red, gold-trimmed Mercedes as he cruised down our street, bragging to the reporter about his drug empire. In his bragging, he must have given too much information because he was arrested a couple of weeks later. In the subsequent news report and in a couple of others that aired later, guess whose house showed up in the background... ours! My mother used to tell my brother and me, "You may live in the ghetto, but the ghetto is not in you."

OVER-KILL

By the 7th grade, I was becoming increasingly interested in boys, and I had a friend who was just as interested as I was. One weekend, my mother, a public school teacher, had a Saturday workshop to attend. She let me invite my friend, Lonnie, over to spend the weekend because my brother wasn't going to be at home either. It wasn't the first sleep-over the two of us had, but if I remember correctly, it was the last. I already knew, without being reminded, that no one else was allowed in the house, especially boys. Still, my mother reminded me again anyway. I don't know where I got the nerve, but I reasoned I would allow two boys to come over but keep them in the backyard.

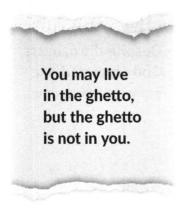

You may live in the ghetto, but the ghetto is not in you.

I don't know if her workshop ended early or what, but my mother came home much earlier than I anticipated. When she entered the house, she called out to me, but I didn't hear her. She walked through our shotgun house looking for me and finally came out the back door. I didn't hear anything because my friend and I were both standing with our backs against the side of the house, locked in long, slobbery kisses with the boys. My mother stood there watching until one of the boys opened his eyes and jumped back. At that moment, God could have called me home to glory, and it wouldn't have been fast enough. After telling the boys they were not welcomed at our house again and telling me in front of them what my punishment was going to be, she had my friend, Lonnie, call her mom to pick her up. The slumber party weekend was officially over. My mother said maybe Lonnie and I weren't the best combination since neither of us made a wise decision. I thought the situation was handled and over with but was I ever wrong!

The following Monday, we visited a private Lutheran school in Berkeley, California, Bethlehem Lutheran School. Before I knew it, with a quickness, I was out of public middle school, and in that private school, along with my five-year-old cousin, Dameon. The school ranged from grades Kindergarten to 8th, but only had a total of sixty students in the entire school. Every boy there was either too young or too unattractive to get my attention, so kissing anybody there was out of the question. Private school didn't exactly fit into our tight budget, but somehow, my mother managed. She was determined I was not getting sucked in by our environment. All this, just for kissing a boy! Is that overkill or what?

Me and Lonnie thinking we were cute in the 7th grade.

Later, that girlfriend, my partner in crime, and I both attended and graduated from Holy Names High School, a large private Catholic all-girls school in Oakland. We both stayed out of trouble, so I guess you can say we stayed on the straight and narrow. She grew up to be a wonderful woman, and we are still friends to this day.

At an early age, I developed this "thing" about not wanting to disappoint my mother. I saw how much she had on her plate, and I didn't want to contribute any additional stress. However, there were times when I'd try to get away with something, but it seemed whenever I did, she always found out. By high school, I had also developed a "thing" about not wanting to disappoint God. I didn't understand it then, but as I said before, I had an image of God's love as performance-based. I wanted to do what was right to earn His love.

PECULIARITY WITH HONOR

In my first year of high school, I realized my approach to life seemed different than those around me. Judging by the things they said and did, I often felt awkward and out of place. I didn't seem to fit in with most of the "popular" kids. Even though some of the things they talked about were uncomfortable for me, there were times I said things that were out of character because on some level, I wanted to fit in. But I never felt comfortable not being authentically me. It wasn't that the other students treated me like they did not like me, or tried to exclude me, but in some ways, we just didn't speak the same language. They seemed quite comfortable with me; the discomfort was mine. I spent many lunch hours in the school's prayer garden praying and thinking instead of eating lunch. Eventually, I embraced the idea it was okay to just be me. I realized later in life, I was

> **I embraced the idea it was okay to just be me.**

never intended to fit in. As God's children, we are called to be different from the world. We are called to be peculiar, and we should wear peculiarity with honor.

> But ye are a chosen generation, a royal priesthood, a holy nation, God's special possession, that you may declare the praises of him who has called you out of darkness into his wonderful light. (1 Peter 2:9 NIV)

CROOKED PATH

Not long after I first began working at the salon in Oakland, I purchased my first brand new car. It was a shiny red Volkswagen Cabriolet drop-top. Life was good—every day was an adventure. I was walking

Graduation picture from Holy Names High School, Oakland, California.

DANGEROUS MISTRUST

closely with the Lord, attending a church I loved, and on the straight and narrow. But things were about to change.

One Sunday morning at church, there was a lot of excitement. A young man I had never seen was there. People crowded around him and seemed excited to see him. I had become a member of the church in his absence. He was handsome, charismatic, and seemed to be loved by young and old. His return was a celebration. At first, I heard he had been away in college, but later, I was told he had been away dealing with a serious drug problem. This should have been a cause for some concern and the perfect time to slow things down and seek God. But I was so naïve about drug addiction, I had no reservations about getting involved with this man. Obviously, he had changed, and I certainly wasn't going to hold his past against him. Besides, he was very much involved in the church and evidently loved the Lord. So, I got into a relationship without seeking God's input.

Eventually, I was a woman in love, and I had a man who loved me, too. It wasn't long before I started letting him drive my shiny, red car. I would even let him drop me off at work for the day and keep my car until I finished. I was in my early twenties, but I really wasn't prepared for all the pressure to compromise my standards regarding sex. I was also listening to others who were telling me, "Girl, if you don't do it, someone else will." When you want to do wrong, the devil will send the counsel of people who will encourage you. The truth is if you must be disobedient to keep a man, he can't possibly be someone God wants for you.

When I made the decision to become sexually active with this man, it was deliberate. I chose to put his desires before my desire to please God. Armed with the encouragement of others and Satan's rationale, we gave in to temptation. It was no accident. It didn't take me by surprise. I couldn't say, "I really didn't mean for it to happen." Yes, I did mean for it to happen. I own it! It was never out of my control to resist the temptation; I chose not to.

No temptation has overtaken you that is not common to man. God is faithful, and He will not let you be tempted beyond your ability, but with the temptation He will also provide the way of escape that you may be able to endure it.

(1 Corinthians 10:13 ESV)

God did not leave me to face the temptations alone, but I didn't choose to do the right thing. I gave in, no excuse to offer.

GOD SAID, NOT SO!

Entering an ongoing sexual relationship was my plan, as I exerted my position as a "grown woman," but God didn't make it easy. As I said before, disappointing Him mattered to me. Every time I had a sexual encounter, I felt miserable. I tried to override the conviction I felt by rationalizing my actions, but the Holy Spirit in me would not be silenced.

My ongoing, premeditated actions were like a weight resting in the pit of my stomach. Contrary to the lie of the Enemy, we cannot say we have repented of a sin if we plan to continue it. We can confess, and even feel bad, but that's not repentance. Repentance requires turning our back on the sin and turning back to God.

I remember my mother describing in one of her classes, how premeditated, ongoing sin (iniquity) will affect Christians who have a heart for pleasing God. She said, "Sin can make you feel like God packed His bags, left town, and left no forwarding address." That was how I felt. There was such loneliness from being out of fellowship. I couldn't pray over, under, or around my sins. I didn't feel God's presence anymore. It seemed He had withdrawn, but it was me who had withdrawn from Him.

Eventually, this man started using drugs again. He kept pretending he wasn't, and I kept pretending I believed him. Then one evening while in my drug-infested neighborhood, he stopped by my house, but I was still at work, and I had my car with me that day. Almost as soon as he stepped into the house, he blurted out to my mother that we were having sex. She didn't even ask him anything. They weren't even talking about sex. Who does that? His judgment must have been impaired by the drugs. Later that night, my mother told me about her conversation with him in a very matter-of-fact way. I think maybe she already suspected something was going on. I thought she could see the guilt in my eyes. She warned me if I continued to deliberately sin and ignore the conviction of the Holy Spirit, by the time I no longer felt any conviction, I'd be in real spiritual trouble. I believed her and decided to end the relationship. I wish I could tell you I ended it then, but I didn't.

WAYS WE CAN NOT IGNORE

The Bible clearly teaches that God disciplines His children.

> Know then in your heart that, as a man disciplines his son, the Lord your God disciplines you. So, keep the commandments of the Lord your God by walking in his ways and by fearing him. (Deuteronomy 8:5-6 ESV)

Sometimes God steps in and gets our attention in ways we cannot ignore. I have experienced His attention-grabbing strategies more than once. One night, my boyfriend failed to pick me up from work. I called him 15 or 20 times until his mother finally picked me up. We drove up and down every drug-infested street we could think of looking for my car. After about two hours, I spotted it parked at a run-down motel. With my heart about to pound out of my chest, I raced from door to door until I found a drug dealer who claimed ownership of my car. He said my boyfriend traded my new car, the one that I had only made six payments on, for a substantial quantity of drugs. He said my car was now his car!

Oh no, he didn't! Even though I saw that this man had a cache of guns and ammunition spread out on the bed behind him, and even though this man looked like a giant standing over me, and even though this man could have dragged me into the room and closed the door, I stood toe to toe with him. I demanded my car back or else I would get the police. He said the only way I was going to get that car was if I gave him the money for the drugs. With every ounce of fury I felt, I told him I wasn't going to give him a dime, and He'd better give me my car back. Or else, what? Going to the police was all I could think of, but I had to get away from that door first. I was talking like I was backed up by a SWAT team. I understand how people do dumb things in the heat of passion that can get them killed.

As I got more animated, he got more threatening. He started threatening to kill my boyfriend. Before I could comment on his deadly threat, I became aware that my boyfriend's mother had joined me at the door. She arrived just in time to hear the threats against her son. I don't know what it was in this man's background, but his toughness was no match for this mother's love for her son. Believe me when I tell you, God used her. The man agreed not to kill her son and did not require any money from me. He reached in his pocket and gave me my keys. But God! I didn't sleep a wink that night. I kept thinking of all the things that could have happened. I cringed as I thought about how boldly I talked to a man who had guns at his disposal. So many thoughts flooded my mind, but one thought came through loud and clear. This relationship had to end, now! And that's exactly what I did.

I realize my feelings about honoring God with my body are unpopular today, even among many Christians. And I have been told, "It doesn't take all that to be a Christian." In our culture, sin is not only tolerated but celebrated. Certain categories of sins are said to be unavoidable. Sexual sin is a prime example of that. I have had people look at me with disbelief in the possibility of abstinence or disbelief in my honesty concerning my willingness to practice abstinence in my singleness.

Obedience is
our love language
to God.

Sadly, the attitude I have encountered many times is that it's unrealistic in the climate we live in to even consider keeping our romantic relationships holy. Even though I haven't always honored God with my body, I never made excuses for my sins, and I have learned the importance of being committed to doing things God's way. Why? I want God's best for my life, so I want to give Him my best. I value a close, personal relationship with Him, and picking and choosing which sins to avoid hinders that kind of relationship. Obedience is our love language to God.

> If ye love me, keep my commands. (John 14:15 NIV)

> Whoever has my commands and keeps them is the one who loves me. The one who loves me will be loved by my Father, and I too will love them and show myself to them.
> (John 14:21 NIV)

MUTE BUTTON

A good honest look at how I handled my personal life provides insight into the main reason I spent years lost in my own personal Maze of Futility, instead of walking the straight and narrow. This was my pattern: when I was attracted to a man, I pushed the "mute button" to avoid the guidance of the Holy Spirit. I threw caution to the wind and scurried off to do my own thing. I would stop spending time in sincere prayer because I didn't want God to intervene in my pursuits, just in case He wasn't in agreement with my plans. If God had not worked so diligently with me, my stubborn attitude could have destroyed me. Yet, with all my mistakes and wasted time in my personal Maze of Futility, I still look forward expectantly because God has a plan for me.

When we turn a deaf ear to God's guidance, whether consciously or unconsciously, we kick wisdom to the curb and walk in stupidity. I am eternally grateful that stupidity does not have to be a life-or-death sentence. Even after making a mess out of my life, I have experiential knowledge that God can turn a mess into a masterpiece and put us back on the straight and narrow.

INWARD APPLICATION

Assess your life. Are you on the straight and narrow, or are you caught in a personal Maze of Futility? If you are caught in a Maze of Futility, what event or events set you on this journey? Do you want to exit this maze? Why or why not? What changes are you willing to make? Give it to God knowing that He wants to set you free.

OUTWARD APPLICATION

This is a tough one! Identify any relationship that is toxic to you: that undercover romance, that person you know has no plans to marry you but is getting marital benefits, that person who makes you feel bad about yourself because of how he/she treats you, that person who treats you like dessert, but you treat him/her like the main course, etc. Pray for strength and let the joker go!

PRAYER

Lord forgive me for my self-sufficiency. Help me to seek Your guidance in all I do from this point on. In Jesus' name, I pray. Amen.

If you are not a Christian or if you are not sure of your salvation, refer to Chapter 10, "The Invitation". If you are sincere, you can be saved today. Much love to you.

Chapter 8

RIGHT PLACE, RIGHT TIME

"I will instruct you and show you the way to go;
with my eye on you, I will give counsel."

(Psalm 32:8 CSB)

Usually, when you hear someone refer to being at the right place at the right time, you think in terms of the physical body being at a certain place at a certain time to gain an advantage of some kind. But the concept of being at the right place at the right time must include having the physical, mental, emotional, and spiritual components in alignment and supportive of each other, to gain an advantage. A missing factor can devastate a situation. For instance, if a person shows up to a marriage with the physical intact but with the mental, emotional, and spiritual components missing, it is problematic. There is a degree of certainty this person is not at the right place at the right time to contribute to a healthy marriage or to benefit from what the marriage could potentially offer.

Being at the right place at the right time involves being prepared to benefit when opportunities are presented. Sometimes, we ask God for things we are not prepared to receive. In fact, if God granted our requests before we are prepared to receive them, we can turn something that has the potential to be a blessing into a curse. Responsible people prepare for what they are asking God for.

REFLECTION

I have been writing in a journal about the events of my life and my feelings about those events for most of my adult life. Some years ago, I began to read over my old journal entries. The more I read, the more convicted I got. I saw how much my mind had been consumed with the desire to have a husband. Nothing else mattered more than that, and I am ashamed of the tunnel vision my entries revealed. I had made an idol out of my dream for a husband and two babies. Not all idols are tangible; some are the intangible things in life such as our dreams, plans, prestige, or status. Anything we want so badly that it takes precedence over pleasing God, takes on the characteristics of an idol. It's biblical to make plans, but we need to willingly surrender to God's authority to overrule or restructure those plans.

Through those old journal entries, I relived a time in my life when I thought being alone (without a man), automatically meant I was lonely. I spent many weekends having ice cream pity parties because I was "lonely." I would eat ice cream and cry while I watched some of my many romantic comedies. I already knew as I dug out my *first* big bowl of ice cream and selected which romantic comedy to watch first, how the night would end. I was going to get more depressed than I already was, cry until I had a headache, go to bed exhausted from the emotional trauma, and stuffed with ice cream and whatever else I ate that night.

During these pity parties, my mind would always go back to my first heartbreak, and I would cry over the love I lost through no fault of my own. I would relive the last time I saw him at the convention.

My pity party nights always included revisiting the question of why God allowed me to get into a relationship that would cause me so much pain. In my heart, I had *erected an altar* to my pain, and I lived in a perpetual state of sacrificing my life to that pain.

In my heart, I had erected an altar to my pain.

My weight reflected those pity parties and contributed even more to my misery. So why was I doing this to myself? That sadness had become my comfort zone and a stronghold in my life. And it seemed easier to keep eating and getting bigger than to do something to turn my situation around. I'd rather wallow in my misery than to fight for something better, even though I would not have to fight alone. I had the help I needed in the power of the Holy Spirit who lives in me and glories in my success.

LOSS OF CONTROL

How was my behavior preparing me for a husband? If the *perfect* man appeared in front of me, I would have been too self-conscious to have a decent conversation with him. My mind would have been bombarded with thoughts of what he was thinking about me. And even if he said he liked women with meat on their bones, I would have either thought he was lying to manipulate me or that he had very low self-esteem to be willing to settle for me. I wouldn't have respected a man whose self-esteem was low enough to want me the way I was—completely undesirable, so I thought.

Don't misunderstand me; there are beautiful, confident plus-sized women who are fierce in their contributions to the world. But my weight reflected my loss of control, and the loss of control was synonymous with failure to me. There was no way I was at the right place at the right time to be in a relationship. Even though I had prayed for a husband, I was not prepared to receive what I asked for. I was not prepared to function effectively in a marriage. The preparation was missing, even if the opportunity presented itself.

In my journal, there weren't any signs of gratitude for the fact that many people I loved were still alive and healthy or that I never had a serious illness. I could afford to live well, drive what I wanted, live a life full of accolades, but my journal entries showed no appreciation for any of those things—no appreciation for life. I was so focused on what I didn't have I couldn't appreciate what I did have. God showed me the condition of my heart in the pages of my journal, and I didn't like what I saw. I was so ashamed and convicted.

I knew I had a problem with low self-esteem, and gaining weight compounded it. Yet, I was just sitting around feeling sorry for myself while getting bigger. A spouse couldn't make me whole when I was so broken. A spouse couldn't make me happy when I was drenched in unhappiness. A spouse couldn't make me feel good about myself when I didn't even understand the source of my value. Entering a marriage dragging a load of traumatic baggage would be unfair to a spouse and to myself. It is a set-up for failure.

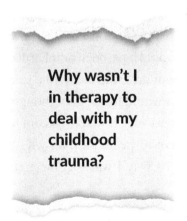

Why wasn't I in therapy to deal with my childhood trauma?

But what was I doing to prepare myself physically, mentally, emotionally, or spiritually for what I said I wanted? There were positive things I could have done to make my life better, but the thought never occurred to me. First, why wasn't I in therapy to deal with my childhood trauma? I later discovered a good Christian therapist is a Godsend. Why didn't I ask God to help me find fulfillment in some other areas of life, at least until I got a man? No, I was so focused on my wants, I didn't care that I had skills and resources that could have benefited someone else. Little girls involved with the Big Brothers and Big Sisters Organization could have benefited from my attention to their needs. I could have joined a gym, gotten a personal trainer, hired a nutritionist, and a cook to address my weight gain. I wasn't even doing anything of substance in the church. I went to church, paid my tithes, went back home, and often cooked a full-course meal and ate it by myself. I could have gotten a puppy to keep me company. Many years later, I got my first puppy, who was great company and comfort for me. Now, I have my second puppy, and she is such a joy. At the heart of my erratic life and convoluted thinking was the fact that I was holding God responsible for my miserable life. If He loved me as much as He loved others, He would do something to make me happy.

WILL YOU SURRENDER OR REBEL?

There is another question I want to consider about being at the right place at the right time. What if your right place at the right time is not God's right place at the right time for you? How do you handle it if marriage, the job you've planned for since childhood, or those children you have envisioned are not in your future? Will you surrender to God's plan for your life? Or will you rebel with a vengeance and accuse God of being unfair—then go hard after your own plans?

As I said before, my life's dream from a young girl was to have a husband and two babies. But as time went by, it became obvious having a baby wasn't in my future, not for any medical reasons, but God never allowed it to happen. Maybe He didn't want me to have any unproductive ties to people He knew would not be a part of my life for the long haul. I don't know. But I had to adjust my thinking and accept that motherhood would not happen for me. Eventually, I became okay with that. I have surrendered to His will over my will.

God can support our plans with little or no changes if we allow Him to influence our plans and goals from the beginning. Scripture says:

> Delight yourself in the LORD and He will give you the desires of your heart. (Psalm 37:4)

I have heard this scripture interpreted incorrectly so many times. It is not telling us God will give us whatever we desire if we delight in Him. What good parent gives a child whatever he asks for anyway? Why would God do such a thing? First, the Hebrew word for delight in this verse means to be pliable, like soft potter's clay, willing to be shaped by God. God wants to shape the desires of our hearts to reflect His desires. He wants us to be open to wanting what He wants us to want.

God must intervene to direct us to follow His will.

That is at the heart of a surrendered life—when we allow God to be God over our lives.

Sometimes God's right place at the right time changes and He is ready to move us to something new. An example is when the Israelites were in bondage in Egypt, they were at the right place at the right time for a season of punishment, repentance, and spiritual growth. But there came a time when being in Egypt was no longer the right place at the right time for them, and God brought them out. Sometimes God allows us to be at a specific place in life until He is ready for us to move to a new place, a new situation, or a new level, which will be our new right place at the right time. However, too often, we resist change, and God must intervene to direct us to follow His will.

STIRRING THE NEST

Some years ago, my pastor, Bishop Kenneth Ulmer, preached a sermon about how the mother eagle stirs her nest to encourage her babies to move on to new adventures. The mother eagle does many fascinating things to direct her eaglets that make her a good example of how God directs His children. The mother supplies a comfortable nest and all the needs to help her eaglets mature. However, there comes a time when the eaglets need to relocate. The nest gets too small and confining, and there's no room for the eaglets to stretch out, to strengthen their wings, and further develop or use the skills they've learned in the nest.

The problem is that the eaglets are so used to their present location, even with its routine, predictability, and discomforts, they still prefer the known to the unknown. Mother eagle understands their dilemma and starts pulling out some of the soft materials that make the nest comfortable until the eaglets can no longer tolerate the thorns and thistles poking them. Eventually, the eaglets get so uncomfortable in their location, they start to vacate the nest and move on to new locations, new adventures, and new opportunities. Mother eagle watches closely as they explore new territory, just in case she needs to swoop underneath them and give them support to keep them from falling.

I can't help but relate the story of the mother eagle to how God directed me to make major changes in my life when I hesitated to leave the old familiar and move on to the new unfamiliar. Since I was a young girl, I dreamed about being a hairstylist. For many years, this was the primary focus of my life, but I had become increasingly aware God was directing me to a new focus in life—one that makes Him, and His Kingdom work my focus. He began this process by making my old, familiar surroundings increasingly uncomfortable, so I would eventually venture out to new, less familiar territory. In retrospect, I realize the Lord was always ready to swoop down and give His support when I was falling.

Following my tour with singers, En Vogue, I was ready to settle down and stay put. After becoming the owner of Eclipse Salon, I saw myself working there until I was forced to retire, and only then, when I could no longer do the work. I hired an energetic publicist and worked very hard until I reached a point where I could truly call myself a celebrity stylist, which was the goal I set for my career.

Because of my success, my salon was featured in national magazines and was voted one of the top 10 urban salons in the nation. In another magazine, I was voted one of the 50 most influential women in the hair care industry. Still, in another magazine, I was voted one of the

Me and a few of my celebrity clients, from left to right, Kellie Williams, Wendy Raquel Robinson, me, Cherrelle, Miki Howard, and Nia Long.

CHAPTER 8 – RIGHT PLACE, RIGHT TIME

top 10 African American hairstylists in the country. I was featured in several other magazine articles, which eventually led to appearances on beauty makeover television shows, and I traveled the country teaching hair cutting and hair finishing techniques. I developed my own, very well received, finishing oil that produced my distinctive finishing shine.

Before reality shows were popular, I was approached to do a show about the activities in my salon. I turned down the opportunity because I wasn't confident enough for that level of exposure, and I was uncomfortable with the lack of content control. All this activity consumed my time, energy, and basically my life. Even though I was always ready to share the gospel with anyone who sat in my chair, that, along with going to church and paying tithes was about all I had time for as it related to working for the Lord.

SHIFTING FOCUS

For many years, God allowed me to use my gifts, and I have no doubts He has supported my efforts and opened doors for me in my career. I owned and successfully ran Eclipse Salon for 15 years, but over the years, my interests and desires started changing. I began feeling remiss in not using the spiritual gifts I knew I had. I was so busy running a business and chasing my career I didn't have enough time for the things of God. Even though I usually didn't work on the weekends, there were so many times I had to cancel my plans and go to the salon because those working on Saturdays were having problems that required my attention—hot water heater mal-functioning, electrical problems, etc. God had already given me 20 plus years of career success, but what was I giving back to Him? My career was becoming less and less important to me, and I wasn't satisfied anymore with it being the center of my life, but I didn't know how to change it. I seemed to be on a fast-paced treadmill, too tired to run on, but too afraid to jump off.

Keeping a large salon working at peak efficiency is no small task. But I had no plans to quit because it seemed like such a massive job to dismantle a business. I would be dismantling my whole life and this life was all I had known for over 20 years. I also felt obligated to continue to provide a quality work environment for the Eclipse stylists who were now like family. But sometimes, God wants us to move to new territories and work exclusively for Him. I would think about change, but I'd get overwhelmed at the task of restructuring my life.

Things related to my business began to change when the housing market collapsed and affected my real estate property. Because I did not seek wise counsel, I purchased some prime real estate through predatory lenders. I ended up losing a one-million-dollar property and another property worth well over half a million dollars. That was the first of a series of events leading to a downward spiral in my business. My property wasn't the only issue related to the housing market collapse. Many of my clients suffered financial losses, also. Some clients, not necessarily those in the entertainment industry, who came every week and spent an average of $200, stopped coming as often. Some were honest enough to say they were going to a cheaper salon or a beauty school. Others did their own hair or resorted to wearing wigs. My stylists were having some of the same issues with their financial situations. As their clientele dwindled, some moved to salons with cheaper booth rent or started working at home.

Maintaining my salon at the level I was accustomed to became extremely stressful and it was draining my savings. Every time I thought I had solved a problem and had a little breathing space, a new one popped up. Everything was breaking down and my repair bills were ridiculous. Finally, I got it! God was preparing my exit from the familiar to the unfamiliar by sending overwhelming challenges one after another. Eventually, I freed myself of the salon and all the stress that went with it. I had a sense of freedom I can't explain but it was invigorating. That was a decision I might not have ever made had it not been for God making my familiar so uncomfortable. He restructured my life and freed up my time.

I've accomplished all I ever dreamed of in my career. I've traveled to exciting places for exciting events. I've met many interesting people and had the opportunity to share my faith in Christ with many. I have always been well compensated for my work, and I have thoroughly enjoyed my career. I am still a salon owner but on a much smaller scale. I keep my staff down to zero. That gives me the freedom to close my salon whenever necessary without considering the needs of another stylist. Although I've had so much more time to devote to ministry, I still believe God is positioning me for more.

He wants us to use our new wisdom to help others.

Sometimes in life, we've been in situations long enough and God initiates changes according to His purpose for our lives. We've learned the hard lessons He has faithfully taught us through our experiences, and now He wants us to use our new wisdom to help others, while we continue to grow ourselves.

DIVINE TIMING

When I think about it, I see a direct correlation between my spiritual growth and the closing of Eclipse Salon. It has the earmark of God's divine timing. Had I closed the salon earlier, I wouldn't have been ready for the ministry God directed me to. There were still experiences I needed to have, and lessons I needed to learn. I wouldn't have been spiritually prepared. Had I started in the ministry before I closed the salon, I would not have had the time to devote to study, prayer, and preparation. I wouldn't have been at the right place at the right time to benefit from the opportunity God presented to me. When the timing was right, even though I was resistant to change, the Lord removed the cushioning around me to make me uncomfortable enough in my situation that I was willing to follow Him in a new direction.

I could view my situation as a loss, but no, it was a blessing. It was just the first step in a journey of radical changes God is making in my life—changes that will position me for ministry. He has taught me hard lessons about life and about Him. Now, He wants me to use those lessons to serve others who are struggling in ways I can fully relate to. God gave me the gift of time—time to be available to Him, time to study and meditate on His Word, time to minister to other women from the Word of God and my experiences, and time to write this book that I have no doubt God told me to write. I couldn't have imagined the joy of having God use me in ministry. Next to being saved, there is nothing better than to be used by God for His glory. I am humbled that after all my mistakes, God still uses me.

For a Christian, being at the right place at the right time is being in the will of God for your life and His glory. You can never be at the right place at the right time outside of His will.

> There is a way that seems to be right, but in the end, it leads to death. (Proverbs 16:25 NIV)

An old hymn of the church says, "Let Jesus lead you. Let Jesus lead you. Let Jesus lead you… all the way. All the way from Earth to Heaven, Let Jesus lead you, all the way."

INWARD APPLICATION

Sincerely ask the Lord to reveal what you need to do to position yourself to be at the right place at the right time for Him to answer your most heartfelt prayer requests. If you are asking for a godly spouse, what are you doing while you wait? Are you living a life that would make God pleased to present you to a godly person? If you are praying for a better job, are you upgrading your skills?

OUTWARD APPLICATION

Prayerfully ask God for directions on how you can uplift your community, better someone's life, or serve more in and out of the church building.

PRAYER

Father, please give my life a new passion, and a new attitude for serving others in very practical, hands-on ways. Please direct my life to areas of service that will be pleasing to You. In Jesus' name, I pray. Amen.

If you are not a Christian, or you are not sure of your salvation, please refer to Chapter 10, "The Invitation". God wants to help you to be at the right place at the right time, for your good and His glory.

Chapter 9

DEAD-END LIVING

"How joyful is the one whose transgression is forgiven, whose sin is covered! How joyful is a person whom the Lord does not charge with iniquity and in whose spirit is no deceit!" (Psalm 32:1-2 CSB)

After the reappearance of my first love, even though I didn't want a relationship with him, I found myself depressed again because I didn't see any potential for marriage. As I was praying, I got caught up in my tendency to blame God for my disappointments. Even though I didn't say the words, the thoughts were lurking in my mind. I guess He got tired of me falsely accusing Him, and I heard Him speak to me, not in my ears, but in my spirit. He had never spoken so clearly before, and it was so real I couldn't deny it. He said, "I did not cause your disappointments; you did! You need to fall in love with Me and develop a relationship with Me, first. I need to become enough for you." This message jarred me at the core of my being. I sat there amazed as I replayed it in my mind.

After regaining my composure, I began taking a hard look at myself and all my dead-end living. Dead-end living is living apart from the guidance and sanction of God. As I prayed, the Holy Spirit began ministering to me at a level I had not experienced before. He showed me I usually set myself up for every situation that had caused me despair. I had ignored His guidance and warnings and insisted on charting my own course. Wisdom to avoid most of the pitfalls I encountered was readily available to me. Obviously, it's God's will for us to operate in wisdom because He told us to ask for it.

> If any of you lacks wisdom, you should ask God, who gives generously to all without finding fault, and it will be given to you. (James 1:5 NIV)

I had the indwelling Holy Spirit ready to provide insight and guidance, but I did not take advantage of His presence. I made choices that had me lost for years in dead-end living. Now, I was tired, worn out, and thoroughly convinced it was all or nothing. I had to allow God to be first in my life.

I was so sure of what God said to me, I vowed to change immediately. Real change involved sincere repentance, accepting God's forgiveness and His love, then forgiving myself for my past, no matter how ugly it looks. One thing I am certain of, not letting go of the past can only hinder my future. If God doesn't condemn me, I must not condemn myself.

> Therefore, there is now no condemnation for those who are in Christ Jesus. (Romans 8:1 NIV)

They say a sign of insanity is to keep doing the same thing, the same way, and expecting a different result. Well, there is no longer any insanity here. I started spending quality time studying the Bible and praying. I didn't just talk to God, but I started waiting for Him to speak back to my heart. The more I studied and prayed, the more I hungered for Him and for His Word. I asked Him to help me understand why I was struggling so much and please let me know Him—who He really is and what He's really like.

I attended a Bible college for a while, and during this time I also started teaching a women's Bible class at my church. This was perhaps the most refreshing period of my life. I made a committed effort to refocus my mind from a relationship with a man and concentrate on a meaningful relationship with the Lord. Before long, I developed an intimate—for real—relationship with God, not that superficial one I had before. There is no power in a superficial relationship with God, and I needed so much more from Him. I needed Him to change me at the very core of who I was. I needed Him to change me from a wounded little girl to a strong woman of faith.

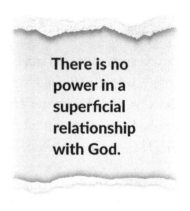

There is no power in a superficial relationship with God.

God assures us that if we draw near to Him, He will draw near to us.

> Come close to God, and God will come close to you. Wash your hands, you sinners; purify your hearts, for your loyalty is divided between God and the world. (James 4:8 NLT)

ON THE THRONE

I took God at His word. I stopped focusing on meeting a man, and I developed a genuine contentment with just the Lord and me. I put everything related to my life in His hand, and I stopped telling Him what I wanted. Instead, I started asking Him to give me what He wanted for me, even if a husband or babies weren't part of the equation.

That genuine decision showed major spiritual growth for me, and I meant every word of it. At no time in the past had I ever imagined life without a man. So, God had finally, after all my dead-end living, gained His proper place in my heart, on the throne! The greatest desire of my life was to be used by God in ministry, whatever that looked like, and I had surrendered everything to Him.

Two years had passed since I began my new walk with the Lord. I was happy, whole, validated, serving, content, and confident. If God never did anything else for me, He had done enough. I knew who I was and whose I was. I had an intimate relationship with a Father who loves me. He gave me purpose, and I was in love with Him.

The burden of low self-esteem had been lifted as I totally surrendered my all to Him. Only God can heal us so completely that there's little residue of the wounds left. Life was good!

DID I GET IT RIGHT?

In 2014, I met a man at church—a six foot four inches, handsome, well-dressed, polished man who was new to our church. I later found out one of his passions was fashion design and the way he dressed reflected that. I was very hesitant to get involved with anyone because I didn't trust my "picker." I didn't want to make any more bad decisions or take any chances on disrupting the beauty of my relationship with the Lord. Other people around us were less cautious than me and encouraged me to talk to him.

As I got to know him better, I noticed he was very personable, and always had time to encourage others around. He would stop by at the end of my women's bible class and the women would stay an extra hour or more to talk to him on various subjects, usually related to relationships. They seemed enthralled by him, and He was always ready to encourage them to "do the work" and to "prepare and position" themselves for what God had for them. That was a phrase he repeated regularly to people. I saw this as an outgrowth of deep spiritual insight developed by an abiding relationship with the Lord.

Being a proponent of Christian counseling, I was impressed this man was a strong advocate for seeking counseling by both men and women. I believe there is a misconception about the role of Christian counseling in the body of Christ. I think our men, especially, see counseling as a sign of weakness. Nothing is farther from the truth. It is a sign of strength

It takes special courage to address the pain associated with trauma.

because it takes special courage to address the pain associated with trauma. So, here was this strong man who was introspective enough to understand the need to seek wellness through counseling when it was necessary. That was a big plus for him.

At some point, he shared with me the tragedy of how he lost several family members in the Jonestown massacre in Guyana, November 18, 1978, and the catastrophic effect it had on his family, especially his mother. Among those lost were three of his sisters. He was eleven years old when it happened and the oldest male in the home. Knowing this event had to be devastating for him as he helplessly watched the suffering of his mother, I asked him if he had received any counseling during this time. He said he had and talked about how it helped him process the tragedy.

THE TIFFANY BOX

Early in our relationship, and several other times, in different settings, he shared an encounter he had with God concerning me. He said God showed him a beautifully wrapped Tiffany box and told him what was in that box represented me—a fragile but priceless treasure. God revealed to him that He was going to show him how to take care of me. Oh, what a wonderful story! I didn't doubt his Tiffany box story because I could easily imagine God, my Heavenly Father, giving instructions concerning me, His daughter. God and I have developed a Father-daughter relationship like that.

I felt God was loving me through this man.

When this man walked next to me, he was so attentive it seemed he was scanning the terrain, keeping a constant vigil, and anticipating every possible danger or inconvenience to me: a pothole, a cracked or uneven sidewalk, a sprinkler that might get a drop of water on me, or a bee that might seek me out. He held tightly to me to avoid any misstep I might make in my six-inch heels. He was a six feet four inches gentle giant walking next to my five feet two inches. I felt God was loving me through this man.

It was the consensus of family and friends I had gotten it right this time. He had a soothing quality about him, as he affirmed and supported those around him. My single friends would say he set the bar high for what they wanted in a man. They enjoyed his presence because he liked to joke and make others laugh. He was just a fun person and had the ability to make people around him feel He really *saw* and valued them. But He had a serious side also.

Although he never initiated any Bible studies, he would pray with me regularly and was quick to pray with others. He also had a prophetic gift that even some pastors said was extremely accurate. When he told me something God had revealed to him, I believed him and willingly

CHAPTER 9 - DEAD-END LIVING

submitted to his leadership. That was a first for me, but I wanted to be that type of woman.

Within the first year of dating, he put me on his 401K plan, health insurance, and made me the beneficiary of his life insurance. Wow! That was a big deal! For the first time ever, I felt covered, protected, and cherished by a man. I wasn't afraid to be vulnerable or transparent with him because he created a *safe* place for me to be authentic. After dating, and being abstinent for two and a half years, I married this mighty man of God who was willing to wait so we could honor God with our bodies.

Even though I had never heard him express any interest in Bible study or teaching, since I was teaching, I *felt* we should do a teaching ministry together. Notice, I said I *felt*. I guess I was still trying to be the *fixer* in some way. But that scenario fit into my ideal image of our Christian marriage. So, when I had the opportunity to switch from teaching in the women's ministry, to teaching in the singles' ministry, I accepted because I could include him in that. So, we started doing our weekly singles' Bible study at church. Later, because of Covid, we did virtual classes.

As I write the remainder of this chapter, I am writing a revised version. The first version took weeks to write, and I was initially very satisfied with what I thought was my final draft. I felt that I had written it with honesty, yet with compassion, and I was ready for the next step in the publishing process. Then on the second day after I finished that draft, as I was preparing for bed, God began speaking to my heart. He wanted me to examine my motivation for writing the first draft with such vivid detail. What was my purpose? Who would benefit from the details? As I was searching for the answer, the Lord put this in my spirit, "You cannot expose all and have compassion at the same time." I realized compassion must outweigh my need for vindication.

Since I know God told me to write this book and gave me the outline for it, I knew He must be pleased with whatever I write in it. I realize even though I could, I can't because God would not be pleased.

UNADDRESSED TRAUMA

This chapter, as well as all the chapters in this book, was written to encourage self-analysis and transparency within the context of seeking, not only to do better, but to be better. My heart breaks for the damage countless men and women suffer, and the trail of destruction they leave for other people because they won't prayerfully seek professional Christian counseling for their unaddressed trauma when necessary. And my heart breaks even more for the men and women who marry these traumatized people who bring all their unresolved trauma into a marriage, which impacts their ability to maintain healthy relationships.

Unaddressed trauma can wreak havoc in the home, not only for the couple, but for any children. In my line of work, I hear so many sad stories of potentially good people, some saved, who are shackled by unaddressed trauma. As I said in the introduction of this book, I didn't write it just for women. I wrote it to encourage men and women who know they have unaddressed trauma and unforgiveness to aggressively seek wholeness for themselves, preferably, before they enter a marriage.

Oh, before I forget, let me address the super-saints who believe seeking help—physical, mental, or emotional—shows a lack of faith in God. Yes, God can and often will perform miracles, but does that mean we just sit around waiting on a miracle? Can't God use people to provide healing and wholeness? Do we wait on a miracle when we are stranded on the highway, or do we call AAA? And even if you call AAA, if you are like me, you are praying as you wait—praying that no cars hit you on the side of the road, or no killer stops first.

Do you wait on a miracle when your baby has a temperature of 105 degrees, or do you use cold compresses as you rush to the emergency room—praying as you go?

There is a problem when you put your faith exclusively in a doctor or therapist, and not in God to work through them. Jesus acknowledged sick people need doctors. Sickness of the mind or emotions is still sickness. Some people experience pain so deep they need help from a therapist or counselor to understand the root of the problem so they can pray to God for deliverance. It is not unusual for hurting people to have erroneous views of God. Maybe they have never experienced love from anyone, and they need a person to walk with them as they learn who God really is, and how He loves them. Sometimes, we just need someone to bare our souls to, someone who will not judge us or be shocked by what we say.

Sickness of the mind or emotions is still sickness.

CRACKS IN THE FOUNDATION

Our marriage started out great, but in a few months, I started noticing some depression, which manifested in withdrawal and increased irritability. Simple statements or requests related to day-to-day living, visibly annoyed him—simple stuff like reminding him of something he said he was going to do before a certain time. This could cause him to react as if I insulted him. His demeanor began giving off vibes, which seemed to say, "The less you talk to me, the better". He started showing a mean side I hadn't seen before. However, I wasn't discouraged. I prayed in faith, sincerely believing that God had blessed the union, and everything was going to be alright.

At the beginning of the marriage, after every problem, he would always come back, tell me God convicted him, and apologize for some mean thing he said or how he acted. He jokingly told people that I would tell God on him when he wasn't acting right, and God would get on him about it. He called me a "spiritual snitch." Iron sharpening iron had to produce some fires suitable for growth, right?

I would take every opportunity to celebrate when he was being pleasant, and there were plenty of times in the beginning. Sometimes I would

post extra sweet messages on Facebook to show him how happy I was when our life was pleasant. And I made a concerted effort to always give him a clean slate because I sincerely believed that our breakthrough was just around the corner. Even in the bad times, I held on to my hope in the marriage. But, as he continued to get meaner and more distant, no matter what he did, or how he acted, he stopped apologizing.

As time marched on, he experienced four other losses of people close to him: his mother, his only brother, his long-time best friend, and his father. A progression of negative changes occurred in his personality after each of these losses.

My wedding day.

He started showing almost no interest in studying to prepare for our weekly lessons. He seemed increasingly more interested in closing himself in the bedroom and playing on his phone. I found myself doing the preparation for the class every week by myself. He would ask what the lesson was about usually a day before the class, and sometimes the day of the class. I would make sure I identified some area of the lesson he could talk about without any preparation, but I was very uncomfortable with "winging" it. Sometimes he would give me topics for lessons, but he took no initiative for the preparation of the lessons, except for only one time he prepared a lesson and took leadership for it.

As he became angrier and more withdrawn, the atmosphere in the home became more hostile and tense. Even the qualities he said he loved about me before we married seemed to be thorns in his side. He would complain about me decorating the house, as if I was slighting him somehow by not collaborating with him before every move. Considering how mean he had become, collaborating was too stressful.

He also started showing anger about what I watched on television, or even if the television was turned to a certain show whether I was actively watching it or not. For instance, he'd walk in the house and get angry because the Kardashians show was on. That gave him a reason to shut up in the bedroom and spend the evening playing on his phone. He could go as long as two weeks without talking to me. It seemed that anything and everything was a catalyst for him to retreat to the bedroom.

Life got even uglier when he started taunting me with things, I shared with him in my most vulnerable moments. Trying to hurt me using information that he knew had already hurt me in the past was a total violation of my trust. I felt myself shrinking into a lesser version of myself as I tried to keep the peace in my surroundings.

We both had been in counseling for two years prior to our marriage—individual and then couples counseling. And we were in counseling all during the marriage, but the problem was, after we started having marital problems, he would not allow me to talk about the real issues in the marriage. If I did bring up something that he didn't want to deal with, the problems got worse. He was never willing to discuss how the traumas he had experienced may have been impacting his life. Counseling will not work unless you work counseling. If a person is not going to be brutally honest with the counselor, he/she can't help you. Counseling is a painful experience, and it's only for those who want to be whole. It is not for the faint of heart. Still, it is well worth it because it can make the difference in your quality of life.

I felt myself shrinking into a lesser version of myself.

We would have a relatively good month or maybe two, and I'd be optimistic the marriage was on the upswing. Then I could say or do something he didn't like, and he might stop talking to me for another two weeks. I may or may not know what my infractions were, or if I did know, his response to them didn't make sense to me. The scripture that says we are not to let the sun go down on our wrath, did not find fulfillment in our house.

From the beginning, he prayed with me before leaving for work, but midway through our marriage, he stopped praying God's blessings on our marriage. His prayers started conveying what he was angry about by telling God those things he wouldn't tell me directly. He seemed to be weaponizing his prayers, but sometimes, those *prayers* were my only clues to what my alleged crimes were.

I walked on eggshells to avoid doing anything to offend him, but I finally figured out that I wasn't the cause of him disconnecting from the marriage. He was doing that on his own. It seemed he entered the house looking for a reason to go straight to the bedroom and zone out on his phone until it was time to emerge and go to work the next day. It was like he barely had energy for work, and nothing left for the marriage or life in general. Eventually, he stopped praying with me at all.

ISOLATION

By nature, I love to cook big meals complete with homemade desserts and have lots of people over. To me, the fun of having a home is sharing with friends and family. At the beginning of the marriage, I was able to enjoy having company over for visits and at times for dinners. But now, I lived in a house where certain friends and family members felt uncomfortable visiting. My husband went from being warm and hospitable to visitors, to being aloof to some and critical and judgmental of others. And when people were visiting, I was always apprehensive he would do something to make them feel uncomfortable, which he did on several occasions. My invitations to visitors came to a standstill.

As new trauma came with the deaths of his family members, I started to notice something that was very puzzling to me. He processed the loss of his family members very differently than I would have. His demeanor showed no outward signs of trauma each time he received the devastating news. I never saw any evidence of tears, no verbal or facial expression of his pain, or any openness to my attempts to comfort him—just emotionless, stoic absorption of the trauma. Was he really that strong? I didn't know what to think or how to help him. I felt I should be holding him and providing comfort, but my efforts were met by rigidity and aloofness.

One day, I got a frightening revelation that eroded the hope I was desperately trying to hold on to. My husband had told me before we were married that he had been in counseling to deal with the trauma of losing his family members in Jonestown. But when we were participating in a television interview the subject of Jonestown came up and the interviewer asked him if he had received any counseling for his trauma. He said no. No! No counseling! Had he been carrying around this unaddressed trauma done to his eleven-year-old self for all these years? How did he cope with it? I never heard him talk about his feelings related to any of the trauma, just the facts. And what about the additional pain of losing four other family members? If he didn't work through it, where did that pain go? Was the pain manifesting in bitterness and anger? I had convinced him to go to grief counseling at one point, but he attended only three or four times before telling me that God had healed him instantly. I know God can heal instantly, but there were no signs of any healing manifested in his behavior, just a steady decline.

One evening, after I learned he had not had counseling for his trauma, we were watching a more recent documentary on the Jonestown massacre. It was one neither of us had seen before. I had the DVR set to record it. As we were watching, a full headshot came on the screen for a few seconds. It was a young woman in Jonestown, not too long before the massacre started. My husband said in a very low, monotone, voice, "That's my sister." The way he said it was so matter of fact it didn't register at first. Then when I realized what he said, I jumped up immediately to rewind it. I was emotional and couldn't believe what I was seeing. Out of the hundreds of people in Jonestown, there was his sister in a screen shot. He hadn't seen her for 41 years and had never seen this picture, which was probably the last shot of her alive, and he sat there stoically without any visible reaction. I remember feeling very sad for him at that moment. How deeply was his pain suppressed for him to show no emotions in this situation that had me fighting back tears?

A WAKE-UP CALL

Initially, I had the utmost respect for my husband's spiritual gifts. But things changed when I started feeling manipulated and controlled by "Thus saith the Lord" type messages. For instance, there is nothing inherent in marriage that dictates I could no longer drive the car of my choice. If I could afford to do so, after giving my tithes and offerings, and paying my other expenses as a single person with one income, I certainly could afford to do so married with two incomes. But me, trying to submit, let my husband tell me God wanted me to be more practical, so I let him talk me into driving a car for two years that I hated. And the car payment was only slightly less than what I paid for the cars I liked. My friends said I was driving a soccer mom's car when I don't even have any kids.

After Covid, I had to close the smaller but still beautiful salon I had opened after the closing of Eclipse Salon. And when it seemed that I would not be able to open again at that same location, I started servicing my clients at their homes. However, that was too much work hauling heavy equipment and products around.

I decided to work temporarily in the back of a Vietnamese nail salon that a friend told me about. Temporarily is the operative word! This was only until I found a new location for a salon. The first day at the nail salon, I had to insist the owner call the roach control company because roaches were running all over the place. I knew I had to hurry and get out of there before I lost all my clients. They were accustomed to coming to a beautiful, relaxing setting, but now, they were in danger of taking roaches home in their purses.

When I told my husband about the situation, he told me God told him He wanted me to stay at that location. Now, wait just a minute! These messages from God were not in keeping with anything I know about God. God has always provided me with the best for my career.

So, now that I am married, God wants me, whose first salon was featured in magazines, to settle into a roach-infested back room at a nail shop? Why would God want that for me? Why would a husband want that for me? And can a husband who is just plain mean to his wife even hear from God anyway?

> Likewise, husbands, live with your wives in an under-standing way, showing honor to the woman as the weaker vessel, since they are heir with you of the grace of life, so that your prayers may not be hindered. (1 Peter 3:7 ESV)

The shop incident was a wake-up call. So, I kindly told my husband my lease was almost up on my car, and I was trading it in and getting one I liked. I also told him I was opening a new salon before I had no clients left. Since ours was a two-income household, losing all my clients was not an option that would have served either of us well. We had a mortgage to pay and two car-notes.

BUT GOD... AGAIN

Once I decided to open a new salon, the God I know swung the doors open in record time. In one day, I found a great location and hired a contractor. The work began the next day after I signed the lease. It included the demolition of most of the inside, a full build-out, installation of plumbing, electrical work, all new equipment, building of storage cabinets, painting the entire place, adding all new flooring, new furniture and other design elements. Everything was finished in three weeks. The contractor worked around the clock to complete the work and didn't even charge me extra. While that work was being done, another vendor, who had stopped doing any hands-on work himself, made an exception for me. Since his employees had full schedules, he not only made me two custom lighted signs for Legacci, but he got up on a ladder at age 88 years old (something he said he never did anymore) and installed the signs in order to meet my timeline. While I was waiting for the completion of everything else, I painted some of my own artwork for the salon. Nothing but God!

Shortly after I told my husband I was changing cars, and getting the salon, I told him we had to talk about the real issues going on in the marriage because it was on life-support. Things were bad, and I started to understand just how bad they were when my only expectation for my husband had been reduced to this one plea: can you just be nice to me? That was the one issue I presented in counseling, my desire for my husband to be nice to me.

There was no single event I can name, but somehow, I had reconciled the disconnect of his emotions. They seemed to have flatlined. I could see emptiness and coldness in his eyes when I asked him if he could just be nice to me. He seemed depleted of what was necessary to empathize with me, to love and respect me, to just be friendly. *But can you just be nice to me?* To avoid another divorce, I would settle for just being able to come home without dreading it so much and making small talk without being the enemy. I would settle for nice because kind was too much to ask for. Kindness comes from the heart, but I would settle for acting nice, until God worked a miracle in his heart.

SUFFERING IN SILENCE

I've been asked why I didn't tell people what was going on in my marriage. Why I continued to do the virtual classes after the marriage started falling apart. Why I sat and listened to him still tell the Tiffany box story when he was mistreating

> I thought the trials were the raw materials for an awesome testimony.

me. Why I did not say anything when he frequently told people we were best friends, when sometimes we hadn't been talking to each other for a week or two. My answer to all these questions is I truly believed the problems were temporary and in due time God would reverse things. I didn't even tell my mother or my close friends. I wanted to protect his image, and I thought the trials of our marriage were the raw materials for an awesome testimony about what God can do.

I also suffered in silence because I was a wife who would not accept the possibility of another divorce. I love the institution of marriage. I love the concept of having an intimate connection with one man for life. I love the concept of an intimacy that allows you to pull back the curtains of pretense, and just be your most authentic self, emerged in genuine acceptance. I love the concept of being privy to each other's areas of vulnerability and covering and strengthening those areas with love. I love the concept of turning a house into a home that brings pleasure and pride to a man. I wanted to be in a healthy marriage, and I was believing God to honor my efforts to make that happen.

During the first counseling session after I insisted we talk about real issues, the counselor gave us a written assignment to explore the issues at the heart of our marital problems. Before we got back for the second session, on the day of my birthday, it was obvious he wanted to start an argument. It was a planned attack and there was no de-escalating it. At that moment, I had a flash of clarity, or maybe I should say a flash of confusion. Who was this man up in my face? What happened to the author of the Tiffany box story? Where was the gentle giant God sent to be my covering and protection—the one to whom God gave specific instructions for my care? I don't know exactly when the metamorphosis was completed, but my husband, my covering, my protector, had ceased to exist. The anger he displayed that night was like his final act of emancipating himself from the responsibility of even trying to be a husband. I could imagine his sigh of relief as he packed his things and physically left the marriage that he had emotionally, mentally, and spiritually checked out of long before that night.

As I reflected on the anger he displayed, my heart is clear that I could not have done anything to solicit his level of rage. I know the facts of the situation, but I don't fully understand all the whys, especially why I ended up in this situation when I truly believed I was at the right place at the right time for a godly marriage. I have searched my mind trying to understand, but all I come up with are questions. Did he come into the marriage having mastered the art of suppressing his emotions under a façade of emotional and spiritual strength? Did the additional trauma of losing family members gradually prove to be too much to suppress? Did pain and bitterness start to spill out more aggressively with each new trauma until there was an eruption that could no longer be contained?

Who was he angry with anyway? Could this anger be directed at God? Was he shaking his fist in the face of God for all his losses going back to his eleven-year-old self? Was he taking God's precious gift (his wife) and throwing it back as a sign of protest? And just in case anyone thinks I still don't know my worth, I know I am a precious gift. I just wasn't appreciated as such. And maybe some may disagree, but I still sincerely believe the Tiffany box story. I believe my ex-husband entered the marriage wanting to be a good husband. I believe that he wanted to be my covering and my protector. I believe he wanted us to be best friends. I believe he wanted to be happy and to make me happy.

THE VOLCANO EFFECT

So, what happened? I believe the pressure of his unaddressed trauma continued to build up until it spilled over all his good intentions and all his plans and dreams, like a volcano spilling lava over the land, scorching, and burning up everything in its path. Naively, I thought I had the "noble" purpose of loving his pain away. How foolish of me to think such a thing, when it took God working through years of counseling to get me to where I am today.

My grandmother used to say, "You can't want something for someone if they don't want it for themself." The same resources available to me are available to anyone who truly wants God's help.

I'm in no position to psychoanalyze anyone, but I can't help but wonder if intense counseling for his many losses would have helped him process his pain and recover. What would have happened if he had taken the advice he often gave to others, to prepare and position himself for what God had for him before he entered the marriage. What if he had done the work, he advised others to do.

I was determined for this marriage to work, until it didn't. Do I take divorce lightly? Certainly not! God hates divorce, but He loves me. Amid being overwhelmed by the divorce, and all the preparation involved in selling a house, God, who is my source, sent me resources in abundance.

My mother dropped everything, made two trips from Arizona to California, and stayed for a total of 11 weeks to push me to get things done. When she caught me just sitting and staring into space, she'd encourage me to get back in the game. In addition to pushing me, God gave her supernatural strength to work like she was half her age, even though she had recently undergone spinal surgery.

My family and friends volunteered in record numbers to help empty out the house, assist with estate sales, and in any other ways they could. And the peace of God that can't be described to anyone who has not experienced it, flooded my soul. He let me know He yet loves me, and He's got me.

AUDACITY

The first Sunday I returned to church after the break-up, I knew the word about the break-up had gotten around. As I was waiting for the praise and worship period to begin, the devil started trying to torment me with self-condemnation, "In this same church, people have seen your marriages and your divorces."

I started wondering what people were thinking. Maybe some, in their self-righteousness, were convinced I had committed the second unforgivable sin, the view that some church folks have of divorce. Maybe some were pitying me because I was alone again. Maybe some were looking at me like I was damaged goods and a statistic for failed marriages.

But suddenly, a calmness flooded over me and the word "audacity" rose in my spirit. My message to the devil is *Yes*, I've made plenty of mistakes I am not proud of. Yes, my sins have displeased God. Yes, I've made bad decisions and entered marriages to broken men, from my own broken place that ended in divorce. Yet, I

I haven't seen the best God has for me.

have the audacity to believe, despite my mistakes, I haven't seen the best God has for me. Like the sentiment of Kurt Carr's song, I haven't seen my best days yet!

I know some people would like to see me engage in some type of self-condemnation, but with all humility, that's not happening. If God has forgiven me, I can forgive myself and move upward.

> Brethren, I count not myself to have apprehended; but this one thing I do, forgetting those things which are behind,

and reaching forth unto those things which are before, I press toward the mark for the prize of the high calling of God in Christ Jesus. (Philippians 3:13-14)

God knew every wrong turn, every dead end, every mistake, every sin that would be in my past and in my future when He saved me. Yet He saved me anyway. He saw my struggles and failures, but He also saw my growth and my potential. Most importantly, He saw my heart. People only judge by what they see, but God sees our hearts.

King David, even after committing adultery and murder, was called a man after God's own heart. God saw King David's heart, and what he saw made the difference. I delight in the fact that God sees my heart and He is a God of another chance. Living under condemnation for sins God has already forgiven you for is the essence of dead-end living. Holding on to the past stifles your future, stunts your growth, and cripples your effectiveness in the Kingdom. God has given me the grace to rise above my confusing past and walk in the confidence there is still better for me and better in me to be used for His glory.

BITTERNESS IS AN OPTION

I am especially grateful to God for not allowing me to become bitter, discouraged, or disenchanted. Some friends have said, jokingly I hope, they wanted to go hurt my ex-husband or tell him off. But I am not bitter toward him, because bitterness is an option we have in any situation, but it is not a given. I choose not to be bitter. We are instructed to pray for those who mistreat us. In doing so, we open the portal for God to heal and bless us. I know God has a call on my life, and I can't have it blocked by bitterness and unforgiveness toward someone in my past.

I sincerely believe if my ex-husband could have done better, he would have done better. My desire for him is that he be healed, whole, and happy, and perhaps have a healthy relationship with someone one day. If he can have a moment of clarity in a mind convoluted with anger, he would know I mean this from my heart.

I still wrestle with the question of how I ended up in a marriage that left me feeling like a PTSD sufferer by the time it ended. What was the purpose of it all? What good came out of it? What lessons can be learned? Who are those lessons for? I do have some answers and some revelations that God has given me—things I hope to share in the future, but for some of the questions, I have no answers. But I stand on God's Word:

> And we know, all things work together for good to them
> that love the Lord, to them who are the called according
> to His purpose. (Romans 8:28)

There are two requirements for God to work things out for our good: we love Him, and we are called for His purpose. Everything is not always good, but God uses the good and the bad according to His purpose. So, when I don't understand His reasons, I can still trust His heart.

To all the people who followed us in our weekly classes, I do feel sad because I know some of you saw our marriage as an image to emulate, but it turned out to be just that, an image, not a reality. To all of you I offer my sincere apologies for any disappointment or pain this situation caused. I solicit your prayers as I move forward in Christ. Please pray for my ex-husband that God may capture his heart and bring him wholeness so he can find true joy in the Lord. I pray over your lives that you will continue to seek intimacy with the Lord and allow Him to work in your life for His glory. In Jesus' name.

Much love to you, Tracci.

> God made my life complete when I placed all the pieces
> before him. When I cleaned up my act, he gave me a fresh

start. Indeed, I've kept alert to God's ways; I haven't taken God for granted. Every day I review the ways he works, I try not to miss a trick. I feel put back together, and I'm watching my step. God rewrote the text of my life when I opened the book of my heart to his eyes.

(2 Samuel 22:21-25 MSG)

INWARD APPLICATION

Be brutally honest with yourself! Are there areas of unhealed trauma or unforgiveness in your life? Refuse to allow it to rob you of your ability to live life to the fullest. Prayerfully seek counseling with a Christian counselor and set on a journey with the Lord to be healed.

OUTWARD APPLICATION

If you have a friend or relative trapped in unresolved trauma or unforgiveness, prayerfully encourage them to seek help. Be willing to be the target of their anger to speak truth into their lives.

PRAYER

Lord, help me to be an instrument of peace to those who are suffering with unresolved trauma, or unforgiveness—to encourage them to seek help. If that person is me, Lord, give me the strength to seek healing and not be satisfied until I have the victory. In Jesus' name. Amen.

If you are not a Christian or if you are unsure of your salvation, please refer to the next chapter. God can do whatever you need done in your life.

Chapter 10

THE INVITATION

"That if you confess with your mouth the Lord Jesus and believe in your heart that God has raised Him from the dead, you will be saved. For with the heart one believes unto righteousness, and with the mouth confession is made unto salvation."

(Romans 10:9-10 NKJV)

I don't know if you have ever had anyone explain to you how to secure a place in heaven before. But you can be sure where you will spend eternity—heaven or hell. To be certain that you are going to hell, you really don't have to do anything but ignore what God says. Some people teach that there are many roads to heaven, or that you have choices of gods to believe in and still get to heaven. But the Bible, which is the inspired Word of God, outlines what the God of the Bible says about the subject.

The Bible teaches that we are all sinners, meaning that we have all fallen short of God's standards of righteousness and are therefore disqualified from going to heaven.

For all have sinned and fall short of the glory of God.

(Romans 3:23)

The penalty for being a sinner is death—eternal separation from God.

> For the wages of sin is death. (Romans 6:23)

There is nothing we can do to alter our destination, but because of His love for us, God gave us a lifeline.

> For God so loved the world that He gave His only Son that whoever believes in Him shall not perish but shall have everlasting life. (John 3:16)

Jesus Christ's death on the cross was an acceptable substitute to God for the death penalty we owed.

> But God demonstrates his own love for us in this: While we were still sinners, Christ died for us. (Romans 5:8)

Jesus came back to life three days later, substantiated who He is, and ensured our resurrection.

> And many of them that sleep in the dust of the earth shall awake, some to everlasting life, and some to shame and everlasting contempt. (Daniel 12:2)

Our salvation depends on what we do with the precious gift God offers us through the death of Jesus.

> For it is by grace (unmerited favor), you have been saved, through faith—and this is not from yourselves, it is the gift of God—not by works, so that no one can boast.
> (Ephesians 2:8-9 NIV)

So, what is expected of us?

> Repent and be baptized, every one of you, in the name of Jesus Christ for the forgiveness of your sins, and you will receive the gift of the Holy Spirit. (Acts 2:38 NIV)

If you would like to tell God that you are putting your faith in Jesus for salvation, you can pray this simple prayer, keeping in mind that the prayer doesn't save you, but trusting God's Word does.

> *Dear God, I recognize that I am a sinner and I rightfully deserve the penalty for my sin, which is death. There is nothing I can do to correct the problem, but I am putting my trust in Jesus, alone, who secured my salvation with His death, burial, and resurrection from the grave. I receive Your gift of forgiveness and everlasting life. Please help me to grow in knowledge of You, and to be productive in Your Kingdom. In Jesus' name. Amen.*

If you believe what God says in His Word, and you put your trust in Jesus Christ for salvation, you have eternal life.

> Very truly I tell you, whoever hears my word and believes him who sent me, has eternal life and will not be judged but has crossed over from death to life. (John 5:24 NIV)

> And I give unto them eternal life; and they shall NEVER perish, and no one shall snatch them out of my hand.
> (John 10:28 ASV, emphasis mine)

> "Now, 'Be diligent to present yourself approved to God as a workman who does not need to be ashamed, handling accurately the word of truth.'" (2 Timothy 2:15 NAS)

Much love, Tracci,

ABOUT THE AUTHOR

Tracci Johnson was born in Fowler, a suburb of Fresno, California. Her parents divorced before her first birthday, and she was raised in a single parent home with her older brother. Her mother was an elementary teacher and later an assistant principal.

No one was surprised with Tracci's career choice because she was preceded by a long line of women in the hair industry. Her fraternal great, great grandmother made wigs for Madame C.J. Walker's company. A fraternal aunt was a celebrity stylist in the 70s and one of the first African American women to own a salon in Beverly Hills. Her maternal grandmother and two of her sisters were stylists and salon owners. Another sister was a barber and pioneered in becoming a female barber shop owner in the state of Texas.

While studying at the Institute of Cosmetology in Oakland, California in the 80s, Tracci was sought by the late Ron Newton, master stylist, and son of the late Black Panther leader, Huey P. Newton, as his assistant. Under his mentoring, Tracci became one of the busiest stylists in Oakland, before moving to Los Angeles to pursue her dream of becoming a celebrity stylist. Little did she know, but there would be many obstacles and lessons to be learned in her path.

After a long unanticipated struggle, Tracci established herself as a very successful celebrity stylist and owner of Eclipse Salon on Melrose in Hollywood, California. During her career, she toured with Pebbles, En Vogue the 90s super group, and Babyface as a key stylist. She also serviced, either in her salon or on sets, such celebrities as El Debarge, LL Cool J and his wife, Simone Smith, Jada-Pinkett-Smith, Nia Long, Wendy Raquel Robinson, Kelly Williams, Elise Neal, Brandy, Kelly Price, Keisha Cole, Natalie Cole, Cicely Tyson,

Tisha Campbell, Tichina Arnold, CeCe Winans, Lynn Whitfield, and others. Other stylists who worked in Eclipse Salon serviced clients such as Janet Jackson, Forrest Whittaker, Terrence Howard, Dr. Dre, Arsenio Hall, Shaquille O'Neal, and other Lakers' team members and many of their wives.

Tracci's talents have been displayed on ABC's *Extreme Makeover* and other make-over shows. Her styles have graced the stages of the Oscars, the Grammys, BET Awards, Image Awards, movies, music videos, and television shows. She has appeared in several publications such as *In Style, Essence, Upscale, Salon Sense, Sophisticates Black Hair*, and others. *Upscale* Magazine voted her one of the top ten African American stylists in the country. *Salon Sense* Magazine voted her one of the 50 most influential women in the beauty industry and voted her salon as one of the top 10 urban salons in the nation.

Although highly successful in business, Tracci's private life was a total failure. The total of her worth was wrapped up in her public image, but privately, her life was riddled with a foreboding darkness, brokenness, bitterness, unforgiveness, self-loathing, pretense, and a constant feeling of not being enough. She lived with the fear of losing her ability to project the confident person she presented to the world.

At the age of eight, Tracci accepted Jesus as her Savior, but failed to grasp the significance of surrendering to His Lordship. Her toxic relationship with her earthly father impacted her view of God, the heavenly Father, and her ability to trust His unconditional love for her. Her *dangerous mistrust* of God left her exposed and vulnerable to the many attacks of Satan as she navigated her life with an often-intentional disregard for God's guidance. Not trusting God was a sin that had catastrophic consequences in her life and ushered in many other sins that derailed her ability to be used of God.

Her life was on a downward spiral until God intervened and taught her the value of trusting Him. She not only found Him to be trustworthy but found in Him everything that she was so desperately searching for. Once she was delivered from her destructive self-sufficiency and mistrust, she opened herself up to God's plan for her life, and in doing so, she exchanged her driving passion for her career for a driving passion to be used in ministry. She not only found her purpose but realized that where God wants her is the most fulfilling place to be.

Instrumental in Tracci's deliverance was her willingness to forgive and release the bitterness she carried against her father. The lessons she learned from her experiences have allowed her to approach ministry with a passion to help others, especially women, from the Word of God and lessons she learned from her own experiences. She began teaching a women's Bible class and later a singles' ministry. Currently, she is the founder of the Ruth Group, a women's ministry.

After a life of pretending to be happy and well adjusted, Tracci values authenticity, and allows access into some of her most private situations in a genuine effort to help others.

ACKNOWLEDGMENTS

I can't refer to an extensive team of supporters who helped me produce this book. The truth is that I told very few people about this project because I didn't want the pressure of having people inquiring about the completion date or how things were coming along. I didn't realize it initially, but I had a very unrealistic view of the amount of time it would take to bring this book to completion. Only after I had finished the first chapter six times, did I understand that it would be a very long process of trial and error.

Even though this book wasn't the result of a big team effort, there are those who have poured into my life over many years, and they certainly share in this accomplishment. First, I want to give honor to my Heavenly Father whose broad shoulders endured my misplaced anger and frustrations, and yet loved me during the best and worst of times. There are many clichés and catch-phrases familiar to those in the "Christian world," but when you experience the sentiments of these phrases, they become more than church jargon. They become heartfelt declarations. One such phrase that took on new meaning for me is, "He picked me up, turned me around, and placed my feet on solid ground." That's my truth—my unfaltering belief about my heavenly Father, and I give Him all praises and all glory! I love You, Father God!

I want to thank my Pastor and spiritual father for the last 35 years, Bishop Kenneth Ulmer, pastor of Faithful Central Bible Church, Inglewood, California. Bishop Ulmer's dynamic preaching and in-depth teaching, not only nurtured my soul but challenged me to grow. Alongside Bishop Ulmer, his beautiful wife, Togetta Ulmer, has served sacrificially to pour into my life and the lives of countless others. Thank you, Bishop Ulmer and Lady T!

Special thanks to my mother who was my first Bible teacher and my life-long confidant. Thank you for always telling me the truth from scripture whether I wanted to hear it or not. Special thanks to you for listening to my raw ideas and providing feedback. And your typing and editing skills were paramount in the completion of this book. I know I pushed your patience with my constant flow of changes, but you made them with little resistance (except for a bit of fussing from time to time or maybe a lot of fussing sometimes). Got to keep it real. I salute you as an amazing mother and a consistent example of Christian authenticity.

I want to thank Pennae' Akpuru and Shirley Strawberry who have walked so closely with me for many years. God allowed our paths to cross years ago and I can stand taller because of the support our friendship has provided. You remind me of who I am in Christ when I need to be refreshed. May God continue to richly bless you.

To my "ride or die" sisters/friends, you know who you are, you are such a blessing to my life—hand selected by God, Himself. You come from all walks of life and entered my life at different junctures, but you all have one thing in common: you are the ones who pray and cry with me in the valleys and truly celebrate my mountain-top experiences. Thank you for setting the bar so high that I am always encouraged that I can and will come out stronger, no matter the challenge ahead. Whether I've known you since elementary school or met you more recently, you are a priceless part of my life. Thank you for your love and support.

I want to acknowledge all the beautiful ladies who attended my weekly Bible class at Faithful Central Bible Church, in addition to the women and men who supported the Living Single Ministry. Your hunger to learn and your desire to be a better version of you has been encouraging to me, and I sincerely thank you for how you have impacted my life.

I must acknowledge my earthly father who is no longer living. Although he was a no-show most of my life, God used our strained relationship to teach me some of my most valuable lessons, such as the importance of spiritual integrity, the importance of forgiveness, and the importance of compassion. I learned the necessity of looking through the eyes of others rather than just my own, to evaluate more than the *who* and *what* of a person, but to seek to understand the *why*. And from the interaction with my father, God taught me that He can use anything for my good—the good things, the bad things, and the ugly things.

> All things work together for good to those who love God,
> to them who are called according to His purpose.
>   (Romans 8:28)

I want to dedicate this book to Ron Newton, son of activist, Huey Newton, and the best hair stylist I've ever known. Ron took me under his wings even before I completed Cosmetology School, and I am the stylist that I am today because of him. He was my mentor and then became my best friend. He poured his legacy into me; then he took his own life, leaving a host of people shocked and deeply saddened. His death is a constant reminder that we need God's help to "look deeper" beyond the facades of hurting people in order to minister to their pain.

And finally, I want to thank all of my faithful clients who have supported me for the past thirty (30) plus years. Many of you have been more than clients, you have been my friends. You have journeyed with me as I transitioned with the help of God from an insecure girl to a confident woman. My many hours of transparent interaction with you have provided the training ground and launching pad for my ministry to women. You all have my heartfelt appreciation for the part you played in my development.

Much Love,
Tracci

Made in the USA
Coppell, TX
27 September 2022